Contents

KU-196-094

Dedication

This book is dedicated to the late David Longworth, the best head of department I ever worked for.

– Keyth Richardson

Acknowledgements

I would like to acknowledge the help, advice and feedback from my wife Sara in producing this book, and the great staff at Hodder.

– Keyth Richardson

The authors and publishers would like to thank the following for permission to reproduce copyright illustrations:

p.1 © Bananastock/Photolibrary Group Ltd/Getty Images; p.2 © Getty Images/iStockphoto/Thinkstock; p.3 top © Andres Rodriguez – Fotolia, bottom © Yuri Arcurs – Fotolia.com; p.5 from left to right, top to bottom © Tatjana Marintschuk – Fotolia.com, © Chantal SEIGNEURGENS – Fotolia.com, © Yuri Arcurs – Fotolia, © EastWest Imaging – Fotolia, © Dmitrijs Dmitrijevs – Fotolia.com, © Bananastock/Photolibrary Group Ltd/Getty Images, © Getty Images/Stockbyte/Thinkstock, © diego cervo – Fotolia, © uwimages – Fotolia, © David De Lossy/Getty Images/Thinkstock; p.6 © Justin Kase ztwoz/Alamy; p.8 left © Getty Images/Goodshoot RF/Thinkstock, right © CandyBox Images – Fotolia; p.9 top © Jeremy Hoare/Alamy, bottom © Neil Tingle/Alamy; p.10 top © Getty Images/iStockphoto/Thinkstock; p.11 © Getty Images/Wavebreak Media/Thinkstock; p.12 bottom © Getty Images/iStockphoto/Thinkstock; p.13 © Ian G Dagnall/Alamy; p.14 © Getty Images/iStockphoto/Thinkstock; p.21 © Deklofenak – Fotolia; p.25 © Getty Images/Fuse/Thinkstock; p.26 © Bananastock/Photolibrary Group Ltd/Getty Images; p.27 top © Getty Images/nPine/Thinkstock; p.29 © Getty Images/iStockphoto/Thinkstock; p.30 © Getty Images/Vetta; p.31 © Getty Images/Stockbyte/Thinkstock; p.33 right © IMAGEMORE Co., Ltd./Alamy; p.34 © Monkey Business – Fotolia; p.35 © Getty Images/iStockphoto/Thinkstock; p.37 © searagen – Fotolia; p.38 © Krzysiek z Poczty – Fotolia; p.39 top © CandyBox Images – Fotolia, bottom © Getty Images/iStockphoto/Thinkstock; p.41 top © dinostock – Fotolia, bottom © Kerioak – Fotolia; p.42 © Phoenix – Fotolia; p.43 © felix – Fotolia; p.44 © Getty Images/iStockphoto/Thinkstock; p.46 © Uranov – Fotolia; p.48 © Owen Franken/Corbis; pp.50–1 © Carl Drury/Hodder Education; p.65 © chris32m – Fotolia; p.67 © Stockbyte/Getty Images Ltd; p.68 © Sam Bailey/Hodder Education; p.76 © John Tomaselli – Fotolia.com; p.92 bottom © Sarah Bailey/Hodder Education; p.93 © Getty Images/iStockphoto/Thinkstock; p.109 © Sam Bailey/Hodder Education; pp.118 bottom, 123 middle and bottom © Sarah Bailey/Hodder Education; p.149 © Bon Appetit/Alamy; pp.151 (except step 6), 152 bottom © Sarah Bailey/Hodder Education; p.163 top © Morgan Lane Photography/iStockphoto.com; p.164 Compass; p.165 © Chatchai – Fotolia; p.166 © Getty Images/Stockbyte/Thinkstock; p.167 Crown copyright; p.168 © Getty Images/iStockphoto/Thinkstock;

Chapter 1 The hospitality industry

Learning objectives

By the end of this chapter you should:
- ■ Know the structure of the hospitality industry
- ■ Know the main outlets in the hospitality industry
- ■ Know the career opportunities in the hospitality industry

What does hospitality mean?

Hospitality means to be hospitable; to look after people by providing food, drink and accommodation. This could include, for example, the provision of bedrooms and meeting rooms in a hotel. In some cases hospitality also covers entertainment.

Hospitality: looking after people by providing food, drink and accommodation

Key words

Hospitality – to be hospitable; to look after people by providing services such as food, drink and accommodation.

Catering – providing food and drink.

Activity

Think of everything you have done in the last week. List all the hospitality outlets you have visited in that time, either as a customer or to work there.

Types of outlets and services offered

The hospitality industry employs nearly 2 million people in the UK. Across the world, it is thought that one in eight people work in hospitality. It is a growing industry that provides excellent opportunities for employment, education and training. The industry offers many different **services** to its customers in a range of different **outlets**.

Services offered

Food and drink services

These are offered by cafes, restaurants, pubs and takeaway outlets. Some of these will be individual businesses, some may be part of a chain and some will be in hotels and other places offering guest accommodation.

Accommodation/guest services

Providing accommodation is a significant part of the industry. It includes all businesses that offer places to stay for those away from home, apart from self-catering cottages. The most popular examples are hotels, bed and breakfast establishments, motels, holiday centres, conference centres and student accommodation at universities and colleges. All of these offer services such as housekeeping, laundry and cleaning to their guests.

Reception

While this is often thought of as just being in hotels, any business that has visitors will have reception services. Their main role is to meet and greet the guests and to find out what they want. You will find reception desks at leisure centres, theme parks, clubs, casinos and sporting events.

Reception services are offered in many hospitality outlets

Key words

Services – working in the hospitality industry, you provide a service when you interact with customers, often face to face, to ensure that the food, drink or accommodation offered meets their needs.

Outlets – places that sell goods and services; hospitality outlets include hotels, restaurants and cafés.

Portering

Porters are usually found in mid-range and upmarket hotels. They often wear a uniform and are part of the front-of-house team. They help guests with their luggage by taking it up to their room on arrival. They also collect it from their room when the guests leave. They are normally given tips by the guests.

Leisure facilities

Many hotels have leisure facilities for their guests. These can include swimming pools, gyms, spas and beauty salons. Some of these will be free of charge, but guests usually pay extra for beauty treatments or massages.

Porters help guests with their luggage

Event management

Many large sporting events need food and drink, and sometimes accommodation, for their customers. For example, the National Hunt Festival in Cheltenham each March is the largest outdoor catering event in Europe, feeding thousands of visitors over the four days of the meeting. The Olympics, the Football World Cup and large concerts at stadiums all require someone to manage the provision of food and drinks. It is becoming more common for these firms also to provide the security, toilets, power generators and everything else that is needed.

Entertainment

This links to event management but also includes nightclubs, cinemas, theatres, bowling alleys and anywhere else that offers food and drink alongside the entertainment. This is not fine dining but cinemas, for example, can make more money from the food and drink they sell to customers than they do from ticket sales.

Gambling

Casinos usually offer food and drink to their customers, and in some casinos the food and drinks are free. This is because, by offering food and drink, the customers are more likely to stay on the premises and keep on gambling. The profit made from gambling covers the cost of the free food and drink.

Casinos sometimes offer free food and drink to customers

Outlets

The industry has many different types of outlets; the main ones are described below.

Hotels

The main purpose of a hotel is to provide accommodation, food and drink. Some hotels also have rooms for meetings and functions.

Hotels include:

- guest houses – these offer bed and breakfast accommodation
- budget hotels – these hotels sell bedrooms at cheaper rates than many other hotels, for example, Travelodge, Premier Inn and ibis
- boutique hotels – these are small but offer a high level of service
- luxury hotels – large hotels offering a high level of service, such as The Savoy or Claridge's
- large hotel chains – these have hotels in many locations around the world, for example, Hilton, InterContinental, Radisson, Mandarin Oriental and Sheraton.

Five different star ratings are given to hotels in the UK. Hotels are rated from one to five, with five being used for luxury hotels. Due to the large number of branded hotels in the UK, however, the star rating of a hotel is not as important as it used to be.

> **Activity**
>
> Find out what it means if a hotel has red stars instead of black stars.

Most hotels open 24 hours a day, 365 days a year, although some hotels close during quieter periods. Hotels in summer holiday resorts, for example, often only open from May to October and close in the winter; some ski resorts are closed in the summer.

Hotels operate in different ways depending on where they are located, whether they are part of a branded group, and whether they have a star rating.

- Hotels have to match their products and services to what their customers want.
- Different pricing policies are used depending on the types of customers the hotel serves.
- The style of the furniture and fittings in hotels will differ according to the star rating. For example, a luxury hotel will be lavish and more expensive than a business hotel, which will be functional and often streamlined. Holiday hotels may offer more entertainment and activities, such as trips out.

Luxury hotels and business hotels are different

All hotels need to provide a safe, comfortable, pleasurable, secure and clean environment that offers value for money.

There are many job opportunities in hotels. Some of the jobs include:

Chef

Waiter (in this book, the term is used for male and female serving staff)

Receptionist

Restaurant supervisor

General manager

Housekeeper

Room attendant and cleaner

Concierge.

Some hotels also have:

- information technology specialists
- marketing staff
- account managers
- event and banqueting staff
- maintenance engineers.

Activity

Name six local hotels. Describe their style and who their customers are.

Restaurants

There are over 65,000 restaurants in the UK, offering a range of styles and cuisines. They usually fall into one of the following categories:

- fast food
- brasseries and bistros
- ethnic restaurants, such as Indian, Chinese or Italian
- fine dining
- cafes
- coffee shops.

A UK restaurant

Opening times vary according to the location, restaurant style and customer demand. Location is an important factor for a restaurant. For example, a fine-dining restaurant has to be in an area that will attract the right type of customers with money to spend. This may be either locals or tourists.

First courses

Salad of endive with Roquefort, chives and walnuts
Oak smoked salmon with lime and horseradish dressing,
served with blini
Half dozen Fines de Claire oysters
Ham hock ravioli with white beans, trompettes and parsley

Main courses

Pot roast free-range chicken, tagliatelle of asparagus and morels
Dover sole pan fried with brown butter and capers
John Dory with chives and ginger crust, aromatic broth
Roast rib of Aberdeen Angus beef with Yorkshire pudding and
roast potatoes
Saffron risotto cake with stuffed tomato, grilled vegetables and
Parmesan

Desserts

Aniseed parfait with ginger bread and spiced port figs
Crisp apple tart with clotted cream and Calvados
Honey roast pear with caramel sauce and cardamom custard
Apricot and chocolate soufflé

A menu from a fine-dining establishment

The design, furniture and fittings of restaurants will match the type of customer. Chain restaurants, such as Pizza Hut, will have the same design and furniture in all of their restaurants, to promote their brand. In fine-dining restaurants the seats will be luxurious and comfortable; in fast-food restaurants the seats are usually small and uncomfortable so that people do not stay too long.

Pricing in restaurants also varies according to the style, type and location, and the type of customer they are trying to attract. Some people expect to pay high prices and will not go to restaurants if the price is too low as they think the quality will be poor.

There are many jobs in restaurants, including:
- chefs
- waiters
- receptionists
- managers.

Skills and expertise needed by staff will vary. Some restaurants (for example, large-volume catering and fast food outlets) will need semi-skilled people, while fine-dining restaurants will need skilled chefs and waiters.

Cafes, coffee shops and takeaway outlets

There are a range of different types of cafes and takeaway outlets. Examples of popular takeaways are fish and chip shops, McDonald's, Burger King, KFC and Subway.

Fast-food chains open seven days a week, and some are open 24 hours a day in busy town and city centres. They may also have drive-ins.

Chip shops and fast-food takeaways do well near colleges, schools and universities, as well as local community shopping areas where large numbers of people pass by

Cafes include popular chains such as Starbucks and Costa, as well as independent cafes and transport cafes

Fast-food outlets have managers, shift supervisors and a range of staff such as porters and cleaners. Small cafes are usually run by the owner and a small team of staff.

Activity

What fast-food outlets and takeaways do you use? What makes you choose these ones and not others?

Public houses

Public houses, commonly known as pubs, provide alcoholic drinks; today many also serve food, such as bar snacks. Many pubs (for example, the Wetherspoon's chain) now provide a full restaurant service and offer breakfasts and morning coffee.

Some offer fine dining and are known as gastropubs.

Pubs will employ:
- a manager
- shift leaders
- bar staff
- chefs
- food service staff.

A gastropub

Bars and nightclubs

In many towns and cities these are seen as part of the night-time economy and can bring significant income to the town. They are different from pubs as they usually charge an admission fee, have strict dress codes and employ door supervisors to control admission. They are aimed mainly at younger people, aged from 18 to 30. The emphasis is often on live music or a good DJ, and most will have a dance floor. In some cases their licence will require them to offer food if they are open after midnight, but most customers do not want food. Examples include the Ministry of Sound in London and Cream in Liverpool.

Contract catering companies

Contract catering companies operate in hotels, restaurants, schools, colleges, hospitals and airlines. Examples of companies that offer contract services are ISS, Aramark, Compass, Initial and Sodexo.

These firms also provide catering for events such as Formula 1, Wimbledon, horse racing and other sporting events.

Jobs in contract catering include:
- chefs
- cooks
- food service staff
- receptionists
- managers
- operations directors.

Contract catering companies provide food and drink for events

Most contract catering units have a flexible approach to staffing – chefs and assistants will divide up the work.

Hospitals and residential homes (the care sector)

Food is important in hospitals and care homes – it can help to build a patient's strength so that they recover to full health.

Dieticians play an important role in making sure patients receive the right nutrition to nurse them back to health and advising them on healthy diets once they leave hospital.

Hospital catering

Catering in hospitals operates 365 days a year, from approximately 6 a.m. to 8 p.m. or later. Patients and residents get a choice at breakfast, lunch and dinner, and most food is freshly cooked each day.

Hospitals also cater for staff and visitors. Some NHS hospitals have high-street branded coffee shops such as Costa for patients and visitors. They may also provide hospitality for meetings and small conferences.

Jobs in hospitals and care homes include:

- chefs
- cooks
- kitchen assistants
- food service staff
- catering managers.

Hospitals have a team of skilled and semi-skilled chefs who do a range of jobs. The catering manager will work with the head chef to make sure patients and staff are served with good, nutritious food.

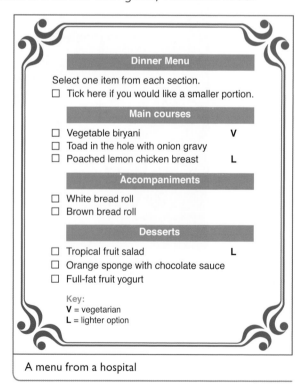

Dinner Menu

Select one item from each section.
☐ Tick here if you would like a smaller portion.

Main courses

☐ Vegetable biryani   V
☐ Toad in the hole with onion gravy
☐ Poached lemon chicken breast   L

Accompaniments

☐ White bread roll
☐ Brown bread roll

Desserts

☐ Tropical fruit salad   L
☐ Orange sponge with chocolate sauce
☐ Full-fat fruit yogurt

Key:
V = vegetarian
L = lighter option

A menu from a hospital

College and university catering and accommodation

Colleges and universities may run their own hospitality outlets with their own staff or they may use a contract catering company.

They serve breakfast, lunch and dinner, and may also run private functions such as weddings.

In college refectories pricing has to be low to suit the students, who are on low incomes; some of the staff may be able to afford a more expensive meal, however, so a range of prices can be found.

Where universities and colleges offer accommodation it is usually in single study bedrooms and these facilities may be used for conferences and events outside term time.

Jobs in these establishments include:

- housekeepers
- room attendants
- chefs
- cooks
- food service staff
- managers
- supervisors.

A college refectory

School meals

Schools have to serve fresh, nutritious food and have to follow strict nutritional guidelines. They may run their own hospitality with their own staff or they may use a contract catering company.

Many of the dining rooms in schools are used for a dual purpose – doubling up as an assembly hall or sports hall.

In some private schools the food compares with many commercial restaurants, as the parents are paying a lot more for it.

Jobs in schools include:

- chefs
- cooks
- assistant cooks
- area managers.

School kitchens usually have a head cook or kitchen manager and a number of kitchen assistants, depending on the style of operation and the number of meals served.

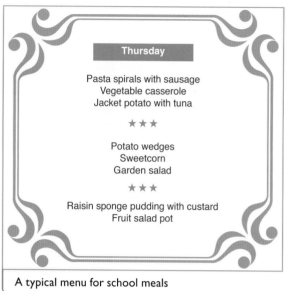

Thursday

Pasta spirals with sausage
Vegetable casserole
Jacket potato with tuna

★ ★ ★

Potato wedges
Sweetcorn
Garden salad

★ ★ ★

Raisin sponge pudding with custard
Fruit salad pot

A typical menu for school meals

Prison services

These provide prisoners and staff with food and drink, serving breakfast, lunch and dinner. Prisoners may also work in the kitchens under supervision, and in many prisons are able to take a professional cookery qualification, which helps them to find work when they get out.

Catering jobs in prisons include chefs and kitchen assistants employed by the prison. As it also provides accommodation for the prisoners, there will also be laundry and cleaning staff, although prisoners are normally expected to keep their own cells clean.

Industrial catering

This is a large sector, feeding people at work in offices, factories and commercial establishments. Industrial catering provides food and drink, and in some cases may also provide accommodation. It includes self-service restaurants, fine dining, coffee shops, food-to-go and snack bars.

Furnishings and fittings can be similar to high-street outlets, offering excellent eating environments. Private, corporate dining rooms in some large organisations serve food and drink of the highest quality.

Jobs will include a wide variety of roles, including:

- chefs
- cooks
- waiters
- food service staff
- managers
- supervisors
- receptionists
- butlers.

Industrial catering: an office canteen

Leisure and tourism outlets

It would be unusual to visit a theme park, museum, football stadium or stately home without finding some form of catering there. This can range from a simple tea shop selling cream teas to full service restaurants offering lunches and dinners.

Theme parks usually offer catering

Voluntary/charity catering

Some charitable organisations provide catering as part of their way of helping others. For example, in many towns and cities, churches and charities provide basic meals for homeless people free of charge. They rely on donations from supporters and businesses to help with this.

In London, the sandwich chain Pret a Manger gives any leftover sandwiches to charities that feed the homeless. Nationally, the Royal Voluntary Service supports older people through lunch clubs, providing food and friendship.

Professional tip

If you want to get involved in charity work while you are a student, see if your college can either organise or support something locally.

Activity

1 Describe how your college catering meets the needs of the students.
2 What changes would you make to your college catering so that it meets your needs? (You cannot lower the prices!)

Stretch yourself

1 Create an information sheet that identifies four different outlets in the hospitality industry.
2 For each outlet, outline three of the services it offers.

Job roles and career opportunities

The main types of jobs have been shown under each of the different types of hospitality outlets. You can see that the hospitality industry offers a wide range of jobs and a mix of full-time and part-time work.

You are likely start your career as a kitchen assistant in a kitchen, or a junior waiter in a restaurant. This will involve working alongside someone who has more experience than you, who will teach you how the business operates. You can expect to be asked to help prepare starters and sweets before you will be allowed to work on main-course dishes. In a restaurant you may start off fetching the food from the kitchen, and then later you will be asked to take orders and give customers their bills.

However good you are at college, your employer will want to see how you work under pressure before they will give you responsibility.

Working patterns

As hospitality is a service industry, businesses have to provide the service when and where the customer wants it. This means that staff have to be there at breakfast (often from 6 a.m.) through lunch and on to dinner (which may last until midnight).

As many outlets operate seven days a week, 52 weeks a year, most staff will have to work shifts to cover these hours. This is usually the case in hotels, hospitals, care homes and prisons.

- Some staff will have to work **split shifts** – this means they work in the morning, have the afternoon off, and then go back to work in the evening. This can be very disruptive for the families of these staff.
- A large number of jobs are part time – this usually means working less than 35 hours a week.
- While some part-time jobs have regular hours, some are **casual** – this means people work when they are needed by the organisation. Casual staff are often used when an organisation needs extra staff for functions and special events.
- Some jobs within the industry are **seasonal** – this means they are only available at certain times of the year when the establishments are busy. For example, hotels in summer holiday resorts often only open from May to October and close in the winter. Some ski resorts are closed in the summer.

Some jobs in the industry are seasonal, such as work at ski resorts

Activity

1. Why do you think there are so many part-time jobs in the hospitality industry?
2. Who will be attracted to part-time work instead of full-time work?

Activity

Give examples of businesses that will use each of the following working patterns (they must all be different businesses):
- full time
- part time
- shift work
- split shifts
- seasonal.

Sources of information on training and career opportunities

There are several ways you can find out about training and career opportunities in the hospitality industry:

- Your college will be able to tell you about all of the training courses it offers, including ones you could do after the course you are on. If there are any other colleges near you, you can check out their websites to see what they can offer.
- Your lecturers will all have worked in the hospitality industry and can offer some good first-hand advice on your career. As they know you quite well they can suggest jobs that might suit you and your skills and personality.
- Springboard UK (www.springboard.uk.net) is a national organisation that provides advice and guidance on careers in the industry.
- Each year organisations such as Springboard UK have a stand at exhibitions, for example, Hotelympia in London or The Hospitality Show in Birmingham. Ask your lecturers if you will be going to one of these. Hotelympia takes place in even years, such as 2014 and 2016, while the Hospitality Show is in odd years, such as 2015.
- Your local Jobcentre Plus will have information on vacancies and training opportunities in your local area. They may have information on apprenticeships you could do after your current course.
- If you have a part-time job already then your colleagues can give you advice, and tell you about their careers and how they got the jobs they have.

Key words

Split shift – where work is split into two or more parts with a break in between. For example, working in the morning, having the afternoon off, and going back to work in the evening.

Casual work – people work when they are required, for example when extra staff are needed for a function or special event.

Seasonal work – work that is only available at certain times of the year. For example, work in ski resorts is usually only available in the winter.

- Local **newspapers** may have adverts for jobs in your area, while **online recruitment agencies** such as Caterer.com (www.caterer.com) have thousands of jobs across the whole country and abroad.
- If you want to work as a chef, the Craft Guild of Chefs (www.craftguildofchefs.org) has career information, advice and competitions you can enter. Ask if any of your chefs are members and if they can help you with a competition you want to enter.

These are just some of the sources of information you can use and, as your career progresses, you will find other sources to help with specific issues.

Activity

1 If you have a job already, describe what sources of information you used to find it.
2 If you are looking for a new job in the industry, what sources of information will you use and why?

Stretch yourself

Plan a presentation that could be given to a group of people wanting to find out about the careers opportunities in the hospitality industry. In your presentation you should:
- describe the job roles available in the industry
- state two different working patterns
- describe three career opportunities in the industry
- identify five sources of information where they can find further information on training and career opportunities.

Applying for a job or a course

Writing your application

Curriculum vitae (CV)

Most colleges and employers will expect you to apply to them in writing, especially if you are looking for a full-time post, not just a holiday or weekend job. They are likely to reject any applications that are not completed correctly or that are poorly presented. However good you are at your job, you will not be interviewed unless your application is good.

The first thing you have to do is produce a CV (this stands for **curriculum vitae**). It is an outline of your educational and professional history.

There are many different ways to present your CV and you can find lots of these online. When choosing the style you want to use for your CV, remember that you are trying to make yourself look as attractive as possible to an employer. Keep your CV brief (no more than two sides of paper) and

remember to add your contact details. If your email address is a silly one that you set up a few years ago, think about setting up a more professional one for your business applications.

Josie Bloggs
57 Smith Street, Hammersmith, London W6 1AB
Tel: 020 xxxx xxx Email: josie@xxxx.com

Personal profile:

I have recently finished studying full time. I am very enthusiastic about working with food. My experience has shown that I am a quick learner and able to work well in a team.

Education:

2012–2014	University of West London Level 1 Diploma in Introduction to Professional Cookery
2007–2012	Fulham Cross School GCSE grade C English language, English literature, Maths, Home Economics; grade D Science, ICT, Art

Employment:

April 2014	Kitchen Assistant, Novotel London West (work placement) I assisted the commis chefs by covering, labelling and storing food safely. I kept the storeroom clean and tidy.
Summer 2013	Apprentice, Hammersmith Hospital (work placement) I assisted with cleaning tasks in the hospital kitchen.

References:

Michala Smith, Chef Lecturer University of West London msmith@xxxx.ac.uk	**Simon Jones, Head of Catering Services** Hammersmith Hospital sjones@xxxx.com

Letter of application

Most employers will also expect a **letter of application** to be sent with the CV. This is your opportunity to show the employer exactly how you meet the needs of the job.

■ Read the information you have about the job very carefully; this might be just an advert, but it may include a job description as well.

■ In your letter you have to show how your skills and experience meet the job requirements. So, work through the job description line by line and decide how you match the job. For example, if it says the person must have two years' experience, make sure you tell the employer in your letter how your experience matches the job.

■ If you have worked in other industries apart from hospitality, you need to show how the skills you learnt there are relevant. If you worked in a shop, you can say how you improved your customer service skills. If you had a paper round, tell them you are reliable and able to get up early and go to work even if the weather is bad.

This is your chance to make sure the employer knows all about you and wants to interview you.

Human Resources Department
London Hotel
London NW1 3BH

57 Smith Street
London W6 1AB

1 August 2014

Dear Sir or Madam,

I am writing to apply for the position of Breakfast Attendant as advertised on your website.

I have a Level 1 Diploma in Introduction to Professional Cookery. During the course I learnt key skills for food and beverage service. This will help me to provide excellent customer care for your clients. I have also learnt about the importance of food safety.

In my work placement at Novotel, I assisted in the kitchen during morning shifts. I showed that I have the energy and enthusiasm to keep up with the fast pace of breakfast service.

Please find enclosed my CV.

Yours faithfully,
Josie Bloggs

Application forms

Some employers do not accept CVs and instead insist that you complete an application form. This is because they want to know the same information about everybody, and it allows them to compare applications quickly. You can use your CV to help you fill in the application form, as most forms will require the same information as on a CV. This is another reason for having a good, clear CV – it makes it much easier to fill in application forms.

- Ensure that you fill in all the sections of the form and do not leave any blanks.
- A poorly completed application form will normally be rejected very quickly. Employers will think that if you cannot be bothered to fill it in, you are unlikely to be very interested in the job.
- Many forms have a section for you to add further information about yourself, usually near the end of the form. Use this to emphasise the skills and abilities you have, and also to add anything that the form has not asked you about. This might include work, activities or anything else that shows you are responsible and willing to learn.
- On any application form do not say that your hobbies or interests are meeting up with friends and socialising, but also never lie on an application by making up a hobby or interest.

Key words

Curriculum vitae – an outline of your educational and professional history. A CV should include your name and contact details; a list all the qualifications you have achieved with the grades and the dates; details of any jobs you have held with dates and what you learnt from them; and any clubs, sports or other activities you have been involved with.

Letter of application – a letter included with your CV when applying for a job; it should highlight the skills and experience you have to meet the job requirements.

APPLICATION FORM

Date	1 August 2014

Title	Ms	First name	Josie	Last name	Bloggs

Telephone	020 xxxx xxxx		Mobile	07xxx xxx xxx

Email	josie@xxxx.com
Address	57 Smith Street

Town/City	London	Postcode	W6 IAB

Are you 18 or over?	Yes
Would you be willing to work unsocial hours?	Yes
Do you have a work permit or visa to work in the UK?	Yes
Position applied for	Kitchen Assistant
Available start date	15 August 2014

Education

School/college (1)	University of West London
Qualifications	Level 1 Diploma Introduction to Professional Cookery
Dates	2012–14
School/college (2)	Fulham Cross School
Qualifications	7 GCSEs
Dates	2007–2012

Previous experience (1)

Role	Kitchen Assistant (placement)
Employer	Novotel London West
Dates	April 2014
Responsibilities	Labelling and storing food safely. Maintaining a clean storeroom.

Previous experience (2)

Role	Apprentice
Employer	Hammersmith Hospital
Dates	July–September 2013
Responsibilities	Kitchen cleaning. Dishwashing. Tidying and storing equipment.
Personal statement (max. 50 words)	I am very enthusiastic about working with food. On my course, I have learnt to prepare hot and cold food safely. I am a quick learner and able to work well in a team.

Activity

List four **dos** and four **don'ts** when completing an application form.

Always ask someone else to read through a letter of application or an application form before you send it off. You may have a spelling mistake or other error that may mean you do not get called for an interview.

The interview

Application forms and letters of application have only one aim: to get you an interview with the employer. So, now you have been invited for an interview, how do you make sure the interview goes well?

The interview

What to wear

You are part of a service industry where a smart, neat and tidy appearance is important.

- Look businesslike for your interview, and men should wear a suit if you can. Charity shops often have men's suits for sale at a low price if you cannot afford a new one. Women can wear skirts or trousers as long as the skirt is not too short and the trousers not too tight.
- Simple earrings are acceptable, but avoid any other face jewellery and do not wear chunky bracelets or large rings.
- Make sure your hair is well groomed and, if it is long, it would be best tied back.
- Your nails should be clean and your teeth brushed. You might like to have some mints with you to ensure clean-smelling breath, especially if you smoke.

Plan how to get there on time

Make sure you know exactly where the interview will be and leave yourself plenty of time to get there. Explaining why you were late is not a good start to an interview, and you might not be interviewed at all if you are late and they do not have time to see you. You could even practise the route beforehand so you know exactly where to go.

What to take

- Always take a copy of the application form, letter of application and your CV with you so that you can read through them before the interview to remind yourself what you said. The interview will be based on these documents so be sure you know them well.
- Read the job description again to remind yourself what they are looking for.
- Take your qualification certificates with you so they can be checked by the employer.
- If you have any letters of recommendation or testimonials from employers, take these as well.
- Switch off your phone.

Questions

You can expect to be asked the following questions:

- Why do you want the job, and what you can offer the employer?
- If you are still at college, you may be asked about your college work and the grades you are achieving on your assessments.
- If you have a part-time job, expect to be asked questions about it, for example, what you like about it and what you would change about it.
- You could be asked about your interests and hobbies, and why you enjoy them. Try to show how the skills you have developed can be applied to work, such as attention to detail, following instructions, teamwork and having responsibility.

You must have planned answers for all these questions and be able to give them clearly.

You will be asked if you have any questions, so have at least one ready, preferably about how the employer sees the business developing. It is not a good idea to ask about breaks and time off.

Activity

List three questions you might be asked by an interviewer and provide an appropriate answer to each.

The outcome

The employer has been using the whole application process to decide who to offer the job to. It will be a mixture of a number of factors, and one you must remember is, 'Will the person fit into the existing team?' Many employers will have a list of factors they consider and will score each applicant for each factor. The person who is offered the job will be the one with the highest marks. If there are several people interviewing the candidates, then the manager will consider all their points of view before making a decision.

Rejection

If there is one job and four people are interviewed for it, then most people will be rejected at an interview. It is not pleasant but you must be ready for rejection and you have to handle this properly.

If you are able to, ask why you were not selected and listen to the feedback from the interviewer. You may need to change something in your behaviour during the interview or your letter of application next time. Do not enter into an argument with them as you will get nowhere and the employer will be even more determined not to employ you. They may have another vacancy in the next few months so you do not want to spoil your chances of a job with them in the future.

> **Stretch yourself**
>
> Practise your interview skills with another student in your group. Take it in turns to interview each other for a job, and then feed back to each other on what went well and what did not go so well.

Chapter 2 — Customer service in the hospitality industry

What does customer service mean?

Customer service is about making sure the customer is looked after, from the moment they step into your business to the moment they leave. It means putting the customers' needs first, ensuring they enjoy coming to your business and that they will recommend you to their friends.

Remember, if there are no customers you will not have a job.

Activity

Working in small groups, make a list of the different places you have been where customer service was important. How did the service you received make you feel?

Good customer service

There are several aspects to giving good customer service. The starting point is to have a positive attitude to your customers at all times. This means wanting to give them a good service and wanting to see them happy. If you do not care about your customers, then very soon you will not have any at all. Even if you are going through a bad time in your personal life, or the boss has told you off, this must not affect how you deal with customers. A professional will always do their best to give the customer what they want.

How do we give good customer service?

First impressions

Most people will make a judgement on someone else based on how they look, and this is particularly true when they are a customer of a business. They will make assumptions about how good the service is likely to be even before they have spoken to you. You must always ensure that a customer's first impression of you is a good one.

Activity

What do you do to ensure customers get a good first impression of you?

As well as being clean, having tidy hair, clean nails and a smart uniform, there are other things to consider.

First impressions are important

Talking to customers

Always greet a customer with a smile and appropriate words such as, 'Good morning' or, 'Good evening'. Some firms have set words for staff to use, but these can often come across as being insincere. 'Have a nice day', for example, is often not taken seriously.

When taking an order from a customer, repeat it back to them to be sure you have heard it correctly. This will prevent problems due to not hearing properly or customers not speaking clearly. In many businesses you will have to write the order down, which can also prevent mistakes. Always remember to thank customers for their business and to encourage them to return.

When answering the phone, always give the name of the business, your own name and ask how you can help. When taking a reservation for either a table or a room, always confirm the details with the customer to ensure that you heard correctly, and ask if there is anything else you can do to help. The more you can find out about the customer before they arrive, the better service you can give them when they do arrive.

Good customer service on the phone is just as important as when greeting customers in person

Activity

What information do you need to have from a customer when they phone to make a restaurant booking?

Written communication

Some businesses forget that the purpose of a menu, brochure or business website is to make customers spend money with them. Anything that is difficult to read or hard to follow will put customers off, so all written communication must be checked carefully. Anything that is wrong or misleading could also be a breach of the law and may end up with the owner in court facing a big fine.

Tips for written communication:

- Do not be too casual – except for some very specialist businesses, text speak is not appropriate.
- An email is the same as any other business letter, and must be spellchecked and have no grammatical errors. Some customers will judge a business on how good the written English is and see poor spelling or poor grammar as a sign that the business does not care how it comes across.

- Where firms send out email or text reminders to customers, these must be businesslike and friendly.

Make sure written communication is appropriate

Activity

1 Search for a local hotel or restaurant website and see how easy it is to use.
2 Does it make you want to stay in the hotel or eat in the restaurant? Explain your reasons.

Body language

How you stand or sit can also give a message to the customer, even if you did not mean to send it. Standing with your hands in your pockets always looks bad and must be avoided. Uniform that is not worn properly, such as shirts hanging outside trousers and skirts, or a tie worn at half mast, is not going to impress your customers.

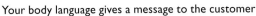
Your body language gives a message to the customer

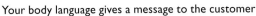

Product knowledge

This means knowing what your company offers and being able to explain it to your customer. This might be about the facilities in the rooms, the leisure activities for guests, local attractions or the food in the restaurant.

A waiter must know what is in each dish on the menu so that, if a customer asks, they are able to explain how the food was cooked and where the raw ingredients came from. In many cases this can be used to help sell food to the customer by emphasising the local specialities or suppliers. If a customer has a specific dietary requirement the waiter must be able help them with their choice of items, or suggest that the kitchen could cook food especially for the customer.

In a larger business it might not be possible for one person to know about all of the products, but they must know who to ask to find out.

Handling complaints

When everything is going well and the customer is enjoying their meal or their stay in the hotel, then it is easy to give good customer service. It is when something goes wrong that the quality of customer service is important. Most people find handling complaints to be a challenge, but you might be one of those who are able to do it well.

Most people do not like complaining about the service or food they have received. If anyone does complain you need to take the complaint seriously. Some firms have a policy that only managers deal with complaints, but in some smaller firms you may have to deal with complaints yourself. There are some key points to remember when dealing with a complaint.

When dealing with complaints:

1 Listen carefully to what the customer is saying. Repeat it back to them to ensure that you understand their complaint.
2 Never interrupt them – it will only make them angry.
3 Apologise that the business has not met their expectations.
4 Find out what they would like you to do to remedy the complaint. This might be to replace food or drink that is not up to standard, or to reduce the bill.
5 Act quickly to remedy the complaint, as the longer the customer is kept waiting the more angry they will be.
6 If you cannot deal with the complaint then get some who can, and explain to the customer what you are doing.

Activity

A customer is complaining that they ordered three starters and so far only two have arrived. Her soup is getting cold waiting for the third starter.

1 Working in pairs, take it in turns to be the customer who is complaining and the member of staff who is dealing with it.
2 How easy did you find it to deal with the complaint? Was it a pleasant experience?

When dealing with a complaint, remember these tips:

■ Do not lose your temper or use bad language.
■ Do not take it personally; it is the business they are complaining about.
■ Do not argue with the customer as it will only make the situation worse.
■ Do not blame someone else, or another section of the business. It is easy for the waiter to blame the kitchen but that does not help to solve the complaint.

Exceeding expectations

When you go to a restaurant you have some expectations of how good the food is going to be and how good the service will be. If it is better than you expected then they will have exceeded your expectations.

Some businesses deliberately set out to do this by under-promising and over-delivering. For example, a restaurant may provide an extra sorbet course, or unlimited coffee at the end of a meal, which leaves the customer thinking they got something for nothing. Any simple personal touch you can bring to help the customer will give them the feeling that you really care about them. In these days of call centres and being held waiting on a phone, this personal touch is really important.

Who are the customers?

Activity

Who are the different types of customers who use the restaurant or other catering facilities in your college? List as many of them as you can.

Some of the more obvious ones using your college catering facilities are students and staff, but you may also have members of the public coming in to. Each customer is different and some of them will have specific needs. For example, they may be hard of hearing, have mobility problems or be partially sighted. A skilled waiter will look out for customers with specific needs and aim to provide the individual service that meets the customer's needs.

A business will have many different external customers

Stretch yourself

What would you do to ensure the following customers had good customer service from you? Be specific and make sure you have really thought about the problems each of these customers might face:
- a blind person
- a vegetarian for religious reasons
- a foreign visitor who does not speak English
- a ten-year-old child in a wheelchair with a carer
- a parent with two children aged under five
- an elderly couple with hearing aids
- someone on a low-fat diet for medical reasons.

The customers described on page 30 are all **external customers** – people from outside the business that use its services. But businesses also have **internal customers**. These are your colleagues – the other people you work with in your own or different departments.

It is just as important to provide good service to internal customers, to make sure things run smoothly, for example:

■ It is important that the housekeeping department lets reception know when rooms have been serviced so that reception can sell them to guests. If housekeeping does not do this, reception cannot do their job.

■ The stores manager needs to work with the head chef on food orders to ensure that they order food in time for when the kitchen needs it. The kitchen must also let the stores manager know of any menu changes, so the correct food can be ordered.

■ The restaurant must inform the kitchen of the bookings they are taking so that the kitchen can order the food and ensure that staff levels are correct.

In many businesses the general manger has a short meeting each day at which the heads of department can be updated by each other on anything that is coming up, so that the guests have good experience during their stay.

If the departments in a hotel do not give each other good service then the customer will not receive good service either.

Different departments need to give each other good service

The benefits of good customer service

There are three main groups of people who benefit if a business gives good customer service:

■ the business
■ the customers
■ the employees of the business.

Key words

External customers – people from outside a business that use its services. These may include new customers as well as existing ones. Each customer may have specific needs, for example a mobility problem or a special diet.

Internal customers – colleagues you work with, both in the same and different departments.

1 Draw three boxes, either on paper or in a Word document, and label them:
   – Benefits to the business
   – Benefits to the customer
   – Benefits to the employee.

2 Put each of the benefits listed below into one of the three boxes:

New customers

Increased pay

Customer satisfaction

Reputation

Profitability

Secure employment

Positive experience

Effective teamwork

Business growth

Improved morale

Exceeding expectations

Accurate and reliable information

Increased spend

Repeat loyal customers

Job satisfaction

3 When you have done this, compare your answers with those of a partner and see if you agree.

4 Do some of the benefits belong in more than one box?

Personal appearance

Personal hygiene and presentation

It is important that all staff look smart and have good personal hygiene. Pay particular attention to the following tips and you will always give a good impression:

- Shower or bath at least once a day, and more often if necessary. This industry can be hot and sweaty, and the customers do not want to smell you or kitchen smells.
- It is best to avoid the use of aftershave and perfume. If you do wear it, choose something that is not too powerful or strong smelling.
- Fingernails and hands must be clean. Short nails are easier to keep clean and look professional. If you are working front of house in a business where nail varnish or extensions are allowed, these should not be too bright or flashy.
- Hair must be clean and away from your face. Constantly touching your hair or brushing it out of your eyes is poor hygiene.
- Clean your teeth twice a day and, if you are a smoker, use a toothpaste that can remove the nicotine stains which can be caused by smoking. Your breath should not smell of tobacco smoke – use a mouth freshener or mints to remove the smell.
- Keep your toe nails trimmed as you will be on your feet a lot and long toe nails can be uncomfortable.
- Jewellery must be kept to a minimum. In a food production area, only simple wedding rings should be worn; in other parts of the business

earrings and other items may be allowed, but staff should always look professional.

Dress codes (clothing and uniform)

Kitchen uniform

Most kitchens will provide their staff with a uniform to wear at work.

Food and drink service

Staff serving food and drink may wear a range of clothing depending on the business's style. Some will be quite formal, others will be more casual.

For staff working in a food service area, all clothing should:

- be comfortable and practical
- allow staff to bend over and move freely
- be hygienic
- give a good impression to the customer
- fit in with the style of the business
- have pockets to hold notepads, pens and bottle openers.

Remember that all employers have to consider the health and safety of their staff, which is why short skirts, high heels and tight trousers are not normally suitable. They can limit movement and may not offer much safety.

Activity

1 Describe or draw the uniform for both an American-themed diner and a fine-dining restaurant.
2 Explain why they would be different.

Housekeeping and cleaning

These staff usually have to do some manual labour, and their uniform should allow them to do this comfortably.

For staff working in housekeeping or cleaning, all clothing should:

- be comfortable and practical for this kind of work
- allow staff to bend over and move freely
- be of a dark colour so that minor marks do not show
- give a good impression to the customer, as these staff are frequently seen by customers in corridors and public rooms
- fit in with the style of the business.

Remember that all employers have to consider the health and safety of their staff, and for these staff it can mean providing protective clothing as part of the uniform. This can include rubber gloves, face masks, eye protectors, ear defenders and safety boots.

Receptionists and other front-of-house staff

It is very important that these staff look professional, and their uniform will be designed to do this. Receptionists are very often the first people a guest will speak to and, particularly if they have had a tiring journey, the first impression is very important.

For all front-of-house staff the uniform should:

- be comfortable to wear – not too hot in summer or too cold in winter
- fit each person properly
- match the style and quality of the hotel
- allow staff to move freely
- be cleaned regularly to remove creases and smells.

Stretch yourself

1 Visit some local hospitality businesses and see how different uniforms are used to give a different atmosphere to the business. Which uniforms really help to give a good image and why?
   (a) Why do you think McDonald's give their staff stars to wear on their name badges?
   (b) Would this idea work in a four-star hotel?

2 (a) Write about your best meal experience and describe what was so good about it.
   (b) How can you use this experience to improve your own performance at work?

3 Collect some local takeaway menus and identify what food they offer that would be suitable for each of the following:
   (a) a Muslim family
   (b) a lactose-intolerant child
   (c) a vegan.

4 How easy would it be for a wheelchair user to use your college catering facilities or public restaurant? Are there any changes you can suggest to make it easier for them?

5 If you were at work and one of your colleagues was being a bit grumpy, what would you do? Normally you get on well with this person and have never had any problems with them before.

Chapter 3 — Serving food and drink

Learning objectives

By the end of this chapter you should be able to:

- Serve food and drink to customers
- Work as part of a food and drink service team in a food service area
- Describe different types of food service

In this book the word 'waiter' is used to describe the person serving food and covers both male and female staff.

Each restaurant and food service operation will have its own specific ways of serving customers. However, there are some standard principles and procedures that are found throughout the hospitality industry. You should be able to apply these to the organisation you are working in. As with all practical skills, the more you practise the better you will become. There is no reason why you cannot be a good waiter.

Personal presentation

In all businesses customers buy from people they like, so you have to make an effort when dealing with customers. Do not bring your personal problems to work – leave them at home.

You can find details on good personal presentation in Chapter 2. Read that chapter and remember what it says.

Activity

Give three reasons why personal appearance is important when serving food and drink.

Teamwork

The hospitality industry is built on **teamwork**. This means everyone pulling together in the same direction.

If you want to be a success you must be willing to be part of a team whose goal is to have happy, satisfied customers and a successful business. To achieve this, you should:

- know your role in the team
- know what everyone else does in the team. This will help you to work together and, if you have to cover someone else's work due to staff sickness or absence, you will be able to do it properly
- phone in and tell the supervisor as soon as you know you are going to be absent or late. They can then rearrange staff to cover your work. If you are unreliable you could lose your job – all service industries need reliable staff
- always follow the instructions of your team leader and pass on messages and information
- be ready to help each other out and always present a united front to the customers.

In many businesses, no one from a shift can go home until all the work is done. In a good team everyone helps to get the clearing up done quickly so that they can leave on time. Anyone who does not work with others will be spoken to by the supervisor and could lose their job.

One key part of being in a team is that if a customer has a complaint, you never blame someone else for the mistake. As all good sports team players know, sometimes you have to 'take one for the team' and, even though it is not your fault, you have to make sure the customer is looked after and their complaint is handled properly.

Key words

Teamwork – working together with your colleagues to achieve a common goal.

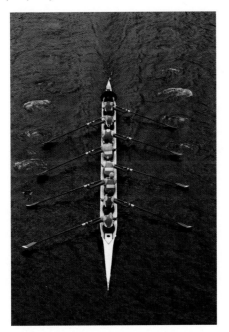

1 Your manager has asked you to produce a written guide to teamwork in your workplace. Create a small booklet that can be given to new members of staff to help them settle in.
2 What could happen if the food service staff do not work as a team? Give three examples.

Stages in serving food and drink

Preparation before service

Always make sure that you know exactly what is on the menu, what the ingredients are and how the food is cooked. Some customers may have food **allergies** and will need to know what they can eat without being made ill. If a customer asks you something you do not know about the food, always find out; do not guess what is in the food. This is very important because people with food allergies may become seriously ill or even die if they eat the food to which they have an allergy. For example, people with a nut allergy may die if they eat nuts.

Always know what is on the menu

Key words

Allergy – an abnormally high sensitivity to certain substances, such as nuts or eggs, which can cause illness or even death.

Check the portion size for each item. This will ensure that the customer gets value for money and that the business works to its budget. If you give too little the customer is unhappy; if you give too much the firm will lose money. Is it one or two sausages? Is it a large spoonful of peas or a medium spoonful? How many chips in a portion? Is it a cup or a mug of coffee? What size ladle for the soup?

Meeting the customer's needs

In a business, each customer who comes in is helping to pay your wages. They expect and deserve a good service from you, and in some cases the better the service you give, the bigger the tip you could receive.

- Always greet each customer with a smile and ask how you can help them. Sometimes your employer may have a specific phrase they want you to use, but in most cases just a natural, 'How may I help you?' is sufficient.
- When you take their food order repeat it back to them as this will show them that you have listened and got it right.
- Serve the customer their food and drink using the correct equipment, plates and bowls.
- When you have served the customer, always check with them that they have what they ordered and that they do not want anything else.

Always check that the customer has everything they need

After service

You will have to clear and tidy up the service areas and ensure that they are clean before you finish. This is all part of being a team member. Leave the area as clean and tidy as you would like to find it when you start work. This will normally mean restocking with plates, cutlery and glasses; bundling up the linen to go to the laundry; and making sure that there are sufficient condiments for the next day.

Clear, tidy up and restock service areas after service

Activity

Write two checklists for where you work:
- one checklist for what should be done before service
- another checklist for what should be done after service.

These must be on a sheet no larger than A4 and should be displayed at work.

Hygiene, health and safety

Apart from your own personal hygiene, there are some other basic principles about hygiene, health and safety to follow. You should check how each of these is done at your place of work.

Cleaning materials

Always use the correct materials for each job. Some of the chemicals used at work are stronger than the ones used at home.

Always read the instructions before using cleaning chemicals, and ensure you use the right **personal protective equipment (PPE)**. This can include wearing gloves to protect your hands, goggles to protect your eyes, and even a face mask so that you do not breathe in harmful fumes. As most of these chemicals kill germs, it is likely they will harm you too if you breathe or swallow them, or splash them on your skin.

One of the most common cleaning materials you will use is dishwashing fluid, which is used in dishwashers – this is much more powerful than domestic washing-up liquid. Never use dishwashing fluid to wash up by hand as you can damage your skin permanently.

Another cleaning material you may use is a specialist surface cleaner, such as D10. It is good practice to use paper towels for wiping down surfaces as these can then be disposed of and not left lying around to harbour germs.

Activity

Produce a wall chart that can be put up at work showing what each of the cleaning materials should be used for and how to use them safely.

As you will have learnt in the kitchen, you need to clean up as you go along and not allow dirty items to pile up before washing them. The sooner dirty items are washed, the less chance there is of microbes multiplying and spreading to other items. Clean items can then be put away, which will help keep the working area clear and tidy. In a restaurant you are always on public view, so it is essential to keep it looking clean and tidy.

Always use cleaning chemicals safely

Activity

Why should you clean up as you go along in a food service operation?

Waste

Waste will normally need to be sorted before it is disposed of. Not only is this more environmentally friendly but it can also save the business money. Each business has to pay to have its waste taken away, so if you can minimise the amount of waste it will be cheaper.

- Glass can always be recycled, as can waste paper such as old menus or wine lists.
- Food waste needs to be placed in containers outside the premises at the end of the shift; these must have close-fitting lids to keep out pests such as rats, mice and birds.

Dispose of waste correctly

Correct use of equipment

Cross-contamination is a constant concern.

- Keep raw and cooked food separate, and use separate serving equipment for each item.
- Ensure all crockery, cutlery and glasses are clean before use, and never put your fingers into glasses to carry them.
- Hold plates by their edges and cutlery by the handles. In many restaurants these items are polished before service, which really makes a difference to their appearance.

Temperature control of food

Hot food must be held at a temperature of 65 °C or above. During service use probes to check that the food is at the right temperature. Ensure that you clean the probe between each food you check, otherwise you could cause cross-contamination.

Refrigerated food should be stored at 5 °C or below, and should also be checked.

Some food on a counter or buffet will be served at room temperature, and this food needs to be carefully monitored. In general, **high-risk food** can be on display for up to four hours at room temperature. After this time it should be consumed or thrown away.

Always keep a record of temperature checks on the forms provided by your employer. If a customer claims to have got food poisoning from your business, a record of temperature checks can show that you acted properly and will be useful evidence in an enquiry.

Check that food is served at the correct temperature

Activity

What are the high-risk foods that need to be monitored on a counter?

Hazards

Anything that can cause an accident could be a **hazard**. Under current legislation, if you see anything that is a hazard at work you must either deal with it or report it to your supervisor.

The most common injuries in the hospitality industry are due to trips and falls, not cuts or burns.

- Keeping the workplace tidy will reduce the chances of falling over.
- It is important to clean up spills immediately.
- Use yellow warning signs when a floor is wet.
- Warn your colleagues of any possible dangers.
- Never use broken equipment as you are likely to injure yourself or someone else. Put up a warning sign so that no one else uses the equipment.

Trips and falls are the most common accidents in the workplace

Key words

Personal protective equipment (PPE) – clothing or equipment designed to protect the wearer from injury.

Cross-contamination – when harmful germs are spread on to food from other food, dirty surfaces, hands or equipment.

High-risk food – food that readily supports the growth of germs.

Hazard – a danger or risk.

What are the main types of food and drink service?

There are a number of styles of food service used, depending on the customer's needs and wants. These are linked to the reason why the customer is eating away from home.

Activity

Write down the number of times you have eaten away from home in the last week. For each time, write down why you ate away from home and describe the type of service you had.

This section is particularly relevant to Level 1 students studying Unit 103 Food service. It covers the main types of food service in the industry and some examples of the types of businesses that use them.

Counter and takeaway service

Counter or **takeaway** service is when the customer comes to the counter to be served their order. It is found in most fast-food outlets, such as burger bars, fish and chip shops and kebab houses, as well as coffee shops and some cafes. It also includes student canteens, many office and workplace dining areas, school meals and motorway services.

> ### Activity
>
> Write down six examples of counter or takeaway food service that you have used recently.

In takeaway outlets and coffee shops the customer usually walks up to the counter, orders their food and pays for it before they leave the counter. They may have to wait for their order to be made up and, if they are eating in, they will carry their own food to a table. The staff have to be able to work quickly as customers in these businesses require a fast service.

In a full meal counter service operation, customers order and collect their own food from the counter and eat it on the premises. Sometimes it is one long counter, but most modern operations use a series of counters so that customers can go to the counter serving what they want and not have to queue behind others. You often find this style of service in department stores, such as John Lewis, and in offices and factories.

Counter service

Equipment

Takeaways tend to use a lot of disposable items as customers usually leave the premises with their food. Before opening, it is important to check that there are plenty of containers available for use.

In a counter service operation, check that there are plenty of plates, bowls and cutlery available, and during service ensure that these are collected and washed up. This flow of crockery and cutlery is essential to keep customers flowing quickly.

In both takeaways and counter service operations you must have the correct serving tools and utensils.

- Each food stuff should have its own service tools to prevent cross-contamination of the food.
- Where customers are helping themselves, you need to keep an on eye on the service tools in case a customer puts one back in the wrong food and it has to be changed.
- In many operations the menu is displayed above the counter so that customers can see what is available before they reach the counter. This means they can make their choice beforehand, and it is quicker to serve them.
- If the menu is not behind the counter it should be at the entrance and be easy to read.

Stretch yourself

Give three examples of what you would do before service starts on a self-service counter in a college.

Table service

This is when the customer is served at their table by the service staff. Four different service styles come under table service but, with all of them, the key point is that the food and drink are brought to the customer by the staff. The different styles are **tray service**, **trolley service**, **plated service** and **silver service**.

Stretch yourself

Write down four reasons why some customers are more suited to table service than counter service.

Tray service

This is used to take food to the customer. It is used in hospitals, care homes and airlines, as well as at hotels for room service.

Key words

Counter or **takeaway service** – the customer comes to the counter to be served their order.

Table service – the customer is served at their table by the service staff.

Tray service – food is taken to the customer on a tray.

Trolley service – food is taken to the customer on a trolley; the food is served from the trolley by a waiter.

Plated service – the customer is seated at the table and the waiter takes their order. The food is prepared in the kitchen and plated up by the chefs. The waiter then takes the food out to the customer and places it in front of them.

Silver service – the waiter serves the food to each guest at the table; each customer has an empty plate put in front of them and the waiter serves their food on to the plate using a service spoon and fork.

In hospitals and care homes the customer or patient will be able to pre-order their food and drink. It is then plated up in the kitchen and taken to the customer with the cutlery, napkins and condiments. It is important to keep the food hot. In many hospitals a special plate that has a built-in container for a heated pellet may be used, which is then placed into a heated trolley. This keeps the food hot while it is being delivered to the patient.

Airlines have their food produced centrally in large kitchens at the airports. It is portioned up and placed on trays and then into a trolley that is loaded on to the aircraft. On the aeroplane the food trolley is plugged into an electrical outlet that either heats the food up to the correct temperature or keeps it chilled, as required. It is then unplugged and wheeled down the aircraft, where the cabin crew serve the passengers.

Most upmarket hotels offer room service to their guests. The guest chooses from a menu and then phones their order through. In some cases these are quite simple meals or sandwiches, and these are delivered on a tray. Many guests like to use this for breakfast as it is quicker than going down to the restaurant. For more elaborate meals the food may arrive on a trolley, which then opens out to form the dining table. The service staff will then set up the table and chairs in the guest's room.

Tray service at a hotel

Tray service normally requires the food to be pre-ordered, although on an aircraft the amount of each item is limited by the airline, and passengers have limited choice. In all other situations, the key stage is checking that the order is correct before it leaves the kitchen. Due to the long distances that can be involved it is not possible to go back and collect items that have been forgotten by mistake. This is normally the responsibility of the waiter in a hotel but in hospitals, where the trays are filled on a production line, there is usually someone who checks each tray as it comes past at the end and puts the cover on it.

There must also be a procedure set up for the collection of empty trays and used crockery:

- In hospitals and care homes this is done at the end of a meal.
- In a hotel it may be done by the housekeeping staff when they service the rooms. Guests will usually put the tray outside their door when they have finished their meal, for it to be collected by housekeeping.

Equipment

It is important that trays are:

- light to carry
- strong, so they do not bend
- easy to clean, preferably by putting them through a dishwasher
- non-slip
- easy to stack.

Many trays are now made of a plastic-type material that can meet all of these needs.

When deciding what sort of tray to buy, the business needs to think about the service lifts the tray may go in, the size of doorways and how heavy a full tray is. That is why room service will normally use a trolley to deliver the food to the room as it will be too heavy to use a tray.

Trolley service

This means the food is taken to the customer on a trolley, and the food is served from the trolley by the waiter. In fine-dining restaurants this may be called **guéridon service**.

It does mean that the restaurant has to be laid out so that the trolley can get round between the tables quite easily. This will limit the number of **covers** that can be served in the restaurant, and this is why it is normally only found in fine dining. One exception to this, which is not usually fine dining, is in a traditional Cantonese dim sum restaurant, when the food is taken round the restaurant on trolleys for customers to pick and choose what they want.

Three types of food are usually served from a trolley.

A **carving trolley** will hold one or more joints of roast meat, along with their traditional accompaniments and gravy. It will have a small heater in it to keep the food hot. This will be taken to the table and a waiter or chef may carve the food for each customer. It is a bit of theatre and makes the customer feel special. When a table has a mixed order of food, it is very important for the waiter to ensure that the trolley arrives at the same time as the rest of the food from the kitchen, so no one is kept waiting. A carving trolley is expensive to operate, as one or two people have to be employed just to look after it. This is one of the reasons that carving trolleys are not used very often now.

Key words

Guéridon service – when food is prepared, cooked or served in the direct view of a customer from a trolley (or 'guéridon').

Cover – the number of customers that a restaurant expects to serve each mealtime.

Stretch yourself

What other reasons can you think of for restaurants not using carving trolleys?

Dessert trolleys were very popular in the 1970s and 1980s and have recently become more popular again. They allow customers to see the full range of desserts available and can help to sell these to customers. Customers may be attracted to order a dessert once they see it. Modern dessert trolleys will have a cold section, with an ice pack or similar in it to keep the desserts cold and safe to eat, especially those with fresh cream or other highly perishable ingredients.

Cheese trolleys are similar to dessert trolleys and allow customers to choose their cheese and biscuits from the selection on the trolley.

For both dessert and cheese trolleys the waiter must know exactly what is on the trolley and be able to offer allergy advice if asked.

Serving from a cheese trolley

If you are using a trolley for service then you must check it is ready before you take it out to the restaurant. Key points to check are:

1 Is the trolley clean, including the legs and wheels, as well as the top?
2 Do you know what is to be put on the trolley, and do you know exactly what is in each item, so you can tell the customers?
3 How will the customer be charged for the food? Do you need a waiter's pad to write the orders on?
4 At the end of service the waiter needs to ensure that the food that is not sold is properly accounted for and put away.
5 Who is responsible for cleaning the trolley down after service?

Stretch yourself

1 List all the items you would check before you took a dessert trolley out to the restaurant.
2 Why could there be more food wastage with a dessert trolley?
3 Why might it be difficult to ensure portion control when serving desserts and cheese from a trolley?

Equipment

The trolley should have sufficient service equipment (tongs, spoons, forks and ladles). Each item of food should have its own service tool to avoid cross-contamination and to stop flavours being transferred.

Ensure that there are sufficient plates to serve the customers, and know where you can get more from when you need them.

If it is a heated trolley, make sure the heater is lit in plenty of time so that the trolley it is hot before you put the food on it. If it is a chilled trolley, make sure it is chilled with an ice pack before you put the food on it. Regularly check the temperature of the food to make sure it is within guidelines.

Plated service

This is one of the simplest types of food service. The customer is seated at a table and the waiter takes their order. The food is prepared in the kitchen and plated up by the chefs. The waiter then takes the food out to the customer and places it in front of them. This style of service is used in a wide range of businesses, from cafes up to Michelin-starred restaurants.

One of the main reasons this type of service is so popular is that it allows the kitchen to arrange the food exactly as required on the plate, giving excellent presentation at all times. This is important when specific garnishes are being used, and the customer will receive the dish exactly as the chef intended. As dishes have become more varied and complex, with the use of more international cuisine in many businesses, it much easier to plate the food up in the kitchen. It is also suitable when a wide range of dishes are being offered to customers, and each has its own accompaniments.

It also gives very good portion control, which helps with controlling costs.

From the customer's point of view, it usually means that the whole table is served at once, so no one has to wait for other customers to be served. In some restaurants the food is covered by a cloche or dish cover; once all the plates are on the table the waiters remove the cloches simultaneously to reveal each dish.

Carrying plated food is a skill, as the more plates you can carry safely the quicker the service will be. You can practise this at home, starting with empty plates and then carrying plates with food on.

If you are carrying hot plates you will need to use a cloth to protect your hands, and you might only be able to carry two plates, one in each hand. In some restaurants waiters use large trays to carry several plates from the kitchen to the sideboard, and then take the plates to each customer individually. This can be quicker and safer with less chance of accidents.

Equipment

Most equipment will be kept in the restaurant and stored on sideboards. This will include:

- cutlery for relaying the tables
- water glasses
- napkins.

Each waiter is responsible for making sure they have a fully stocked sideboard, and for keeping it topped up during service.

Stretch yourself

Name two advantages of using plated service in a restaurant.

Silver service

This is when the waiter serves food to each guest at the table. It was the style of service used in large private houses – you might have seen it in the television series *Downton Abbey*.

Historically all the equipment used for this type of service was silver, but now much of it is stainless steel. It is still used when the customers are all having the same food, as in a banquet, but it has become less popular in restaurants.

With silver service each customer has an empty plate put in front of them and the waiter serves their food on to the plate. The key skill you need is to be able to use a service spoon and fork, as this is how you serve the food from the flat or dish on to the customer's plate.

You will only get this skill though practice, so have a go at home, trying to pick up and serve food. For some items you might find it easier to use two service forks or two fish knives, especially for items such as omelettes or fillets of fish. The skill is ensuring that the food looks good on the customer's plate. If you get it wrong it will look a mess and be unattractive.

Using a service spoon and fork

1 The service fork should be positioned above, or on top of, the service spoon. The key to developing this skill is the locking of the ends of the service spoon and fork with the small finger and the third finger.

2 The spoon and fork are manoeuvred with the thumb and the index and second fingers. Using this method, food items may be picked up from the serving dish in between the service spoon and service fork.

3 Alternatively, the service fork may be turned to mould with the shape of the items being served, for example when serving bread rolls.

As the food will be getting cold all the time it is out of the kitchen, the waiter has to work very quickly to serve it while it is hot. As there could be at least five items to serve to each customer (for example, meat, potatoes, two vegetables and a sauce), waiters will work in a team to serve each table. One will serve the meat, another will serve the potatoes and another will serve the vegetables. This works well when all the customers are eating the same meal; if everyone on a table of eight is having a different dish, however, it will take a long time to serve the whole table and some food will be getting cold.

Another reason why silver service is not used as much as it was in fine-dining restaurants is that there are some dishes that do not look attractive on the plate when served in this way.

1 Explain what sorts of food would not be suitable for silver service.
2 Explain why many fine-dining restaurants use plated service instead of silver service these days.

Equipment

Silver service needs a lot of equipment, and much of this will need to be stored in the kitchen. There must be a range of oval flats in different sizes for meat, fish and poultry to be served on, and a variety of vegetable dishes, which may be split into sections so that two or more vegetables can be served from the same dish.

The waiters will need to have plenty of service spoons and forks in the restaurant to ensure that clean items are used each time. There will normally be a range of sauce boats for serving gravy and other sauces.

Chapter 4 | Basic food preparation and cooking

Learning objectives

By the end of this chapter you should be able to:
- Know the principal methods of cooking
- Choose the correct equipment and use it safely and hygienically
- Select the correct ingredients for basic dishes
- Prepare food items for either cold presentation or for cooking using wet and dry methods
- Cook and present basic food items and simple dishes
- Store prepared food items according to instructions
- Clean work areas and equipment safely and hygienically, during and after food preparation

The main cookery methods

There are eleven main cookery methods, which are described below. These are: boiling, poaching, steaming, stewing, braising, baking, roasting, grilling, deep frying, shallow frying and microwaving.

Recipes are found at the end of this chapter, as many recipes use more than one cooking method.

Boiling

Boiling is when food is covered in liquid (such as water or stock) that is heated up until the liquid starts to bubble vigorously. At this point it is boiling. Usually the heat is then turned down so that the liquid is just bubbling gently.

Boiling is a healthy method of cookery as it does not use any fat and, when done properly, will keep the flavour and nutritional value of the food.

There are two ways of boiling:

1 Place the food in boiling liquid. The liquid will stop boiling when you put the food in, so heat it up to bring it back to boiling, then reduce the heat so that the liquid just bubbles gently (this is known as simmering) and cooks the food.

2 Cover food with cold liquid. Heat it up and bring it to the boil, then reduce the heat to allow the food to simmer.

Foods that can be boiled

The following foods can be boiled successfully:

- meat and poultry
- vegetables
- eggs
- pasta
- pulses and grains.

Liquids used when boiling

The following liquids are usually used when boiling:

- water
- milk
- stock (fresh or a convenience product such as stock cubes).

Boiling

The amount or type of liquid used depends on the type of food being boiled.

Temperature and time control

Temperature must be controlled so that the liquid is brought to the boil and then adjusted to a gentle boil (simmer) until the food is cooked.

The time taken to cook food by boiling depends on the food being cooked:

- Stocks, soups and sauces must only simmer.
- Pasta should not be overcooked but left slightly firm (called *al dente*).
- Meat and poultry should be well cooked and tender.
- Vegetables should not be overcooked but left slightly crisp.

Health and safety

- Lower food gently into boiling water to prevent splashing and scalding.
- Make sure that the handles on pots of boiling liquids are turned in when on stoves, so that sleeves and hands do not catch them.
- When removing the lid from a cooking pot, tilt it away from your face to allow the steam to escape safely. If you open it towards you the hot steam may burn you.

Equipment

Saucepans of various sizes can be used for boiling. Always choose a pan that is the correct size for the item to be boiled – neither too small nor too large. Ensuring that the cooking pot is large enough for the water to cover the food without spilling over the edge once the water starts to boil will reduce the risk of being splashed by boiling water.

Health and safety

Check the cleanliness and condition of the pan before use so as not to cause cross-contamination.

Poaching

Poaching is when food is cooked in a liquid that is very hot but not boiling. It should be just below boiling point.

Foods that can be poached

The following foods can be poached successfully:

- chicken
- eggs
- fish
- fruit.

Liquids used when poaching

The same liquids used for boiling foods can be used when poaching, with a few additions:

- **water** – eggs are usually poached in water, with a little vinegar added
- **milk** – fish fillets, such as smoked haddock, may be poached in milk
- **stock** – the stock should be suited to the food; for example, fish fillets can be poached in fish or vegetable stock and chicken breast fillets in chicken or vegetable stock
- **wine** – fruit, such as pears, may be poached in wine
- **stock syrup** – this is sugar based and normally used for poaching fruit.

Health and safety

Although poaching liquids are not quite as dangerous as boiling liquids, they are still very hot and can cause serious burns or scalds. Be wary of pans of hot liquids – when you lower food into the poaching liquid, you should do so carefully to prevent splashes.

Methods of poaching

For most foods, the poaching liquid is heated first. When it reaches the right temperature, lower the prepared food into the barely simmering liquid and allow it to cook in the gentle heat.

There are two ways of poaching:

1 **Shallow poaching** – cook the food in only a small amount of liquid and cover it with greased greaseproof paper. Never allow the liquid to boil – keep it at a temperature as near to boiling as possible without actually boiling. To prevent the liquid from boiling, bring it to the boil on top of the stove, take it off the direct heat and then place the food in the water. Complete the cooking in a moderately hot oven (approximately 180 °C). Foods poached using this method include cuts of fish, chicken and fruit.

Poaching

2 **Deep poaching** – this can be used to cook eggs. Place eggs in approximately 8 cm of gently simmering water. You can also deep poach whole fish (such as salmon), slices of fish on the bone (such as turbot), filleted cod and salmon, and whole chicken as well as whole fruits. All of these should be covered with the poaching liquid.

Temperature and time control

The temperature must be controlled so that the cooking liquid does not become too cool or too hot. Poaching is cooking at just below simmering point.

It is important to time the cooking correctly so that food is neither undercooked nor overcooked. If it is undercooked it will not be pleasant to eat and can sometimes be dangerous (for example, undercooked chicken). If it is overcooked it will break up and lose some of its nutrients.

The time and temperature needed to cook the food correctly will vary for different types of food.

Equipment

A poaching pan should be used for this method of cooking. A spider, fish slice or slotted spoon can be used to remove poached items from the poaching liquid.

Steaming

Food is cooked in the steam produced by a boiling liquid (rather than placing the food itself in the boiling liquid). It cooks food in a way that keeps most of the nutrients in the food, as none can be lost into the cooking liquor, and it makes some foods lighter and easier to digest.

Foods that can be steamed

The following foods can be steamed successfully:

- chicken
- fish
- vegetables
- savoury and sweet puddings.

Liquids used when steaming

The following liquids can all be used to create a steam in which to cook food:

- water
- stock.

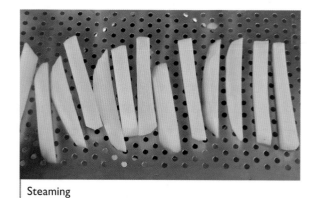

Steaming

Methods and equipment

There are two main methods of steaming:

1 **Atmospheric steaming** – this is a low-pressure steaming method in which steam is produced by placing water in the bottom of a saucepan and bringing it to a rapid boil. Food is placed in a container above the boiling water. The steam from the boiling water heats the container and cooks the food inside it.

2 **High-pressure steaming** – this is done in high-pressure steamers such as pressure cookers. The high pressure in the steamer produces higher temperatures, which cooks the food faster.

> **Professional tip**
>
> High-pressure steaming enables food to be cooked or reheated quickly. It is often used for 'batch' cooking, where small quantities of vegetables are cooked frequently throughout the service. This ensures that the vegetables are always freshly cooked and so they keep their colour, flavour and nutritional content.

Temperature and time control

When using steamers it is important to make sure that the food is not undercooked or overcooked, and therefore that the correct temperature and cooking time is used.

Food cooks much faster in high-pressure steamers and therefore there is a great danger of the food overcooking very quickly. When you are using a high-pressure steamer, wait until the pressure gauge shows that it has reached the correct pressure, then open the door very carefully to allow the steam to escape before you place the food in the steamer. This way you will be sure that the necessary cooking temperature has been reached.

Individual sponge puddings, for example, will cook in less time than when cooking in a large pudding basin to be portioned when cooked.

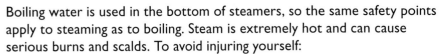

Health and safety

Boiling water is used in the bottom of steamers, so the same safety points apply to steaming as to boiling. Steam is extremely hot and can cause serious burns and scalds. To avoid injuring yourself:

- Make sure you know how to use steamers properly and use them with great care.
- Check the pressure in high-pressure steamers continually and allow the pressure to return to the correct level before opening doors or removing pressure-cooker lids.
- Allow time for the pressure to return to normal before opening commercial steamers. Stand well away from the door as you open it to avoid the full impact of the escaping steam.

Quality points for boiling, poaching and steaming foods

To ensure the quality of finished dishes there are a number of things that a chef should do to ensure the dish meets the customer's expectations:

- **Selection of products** – ensure that products are fresh, have a good appearance, smell as expected and are at the appropriate temperature.
- **Preparation** – foods should be trimmed, shaped and sized according to dish requirements.
- **Cooking process** – the temperature and cooking time should be checked, as should the amount of liquid to be used. These elements will impact on the flavour, colour, texture and taste of the dish.
- **Finishing of the final dish** – consistency, appearance, portion size, seasoning and garnish, if required, should all be considered.

1 Briefly describe the process for the following methods of cooking:
   a poaching
   b steaming
   c boiling.
2 List three vegetables that can be cooked in boiling water.
3 List three types of food that could be steamed.
4 List five safety points for chefs to consider when cooking by boiling, poaching or steaming.
5 List four foods that can be cooked by poaching.
6 Describe one method of boiling.

Stewing

Stewing is a slow, gentle, moist-heat method of cooking in which the food is completely covered by a liquid. Both the food and the sauce are served together. Stews are cooked on top of the stove. Stewing is an ideal method for cheaper cuts of meat and poultry as they often have more flavour than more tender cuts of meat. During stewing, any vitamins, minerals and other nutrients that leach from the food during cooking stay in the liquid and are not lost. When stews are cooked in the oven they are called casseroles.

Foods that can be stewed

The following foods can be stewed successfully:

- meat
- poultry
- fish
- vegetables
- fruit.

Liquids used for stewing

The following liquids may be used for stewing:

- **stock** – savoury items are usually cooked in a stock
- **stock syrup** – a water and sugar base, which can be infused with herbs and spices for cooking fruits in
- **wine** – the alcohol cooks off to leave a rich flavoured sauce to cook meat in
- **beer and cider** – used in the same way as wine, but often associated with regional dishes; these add flavour to the dish
- **sauce** – this includes ready-made sauces, for example velouté, or even convenience sauces such as a curry sauce.

Liquids are added to stews at various points through the cooking process, depending on the recipe. Some are thickened during the cooking process; others are thickened once the main ingredient is cooked, as in a blanquette.

If stews and casseroles are cooked correctly, very little liquid will evaporate, leaving plenty of sauce to serve up as part of the stew. The amount of liquid used should be enough to cover the food items to keep them moist throughout the process. Consistency should be monitored to ensure that there is sufficient liquid/sauce for each portion of the finished dish.

Temperature and time control

Time required will vary according to the type and quantity of foods to be stewed. As a guide, red meat will need longer than poultry, and some vegetables will take longer than fruits.

Good stews are cooked slowly, so it is important to control the temperature properly. The liquid must barely simmer. Use a tight-fitting lid to keep in the steam. This helps to keep the temperature correct and reduces evaporation.

Stewing

Methods

Stews can be cooked on a hob or in an oven depending on the recipe and foods being cooked.

When cooked on a hob, meat and vegetables are placed in a saucepan and covered with liquid (water or stock). The liquid is brought to the boil then turned down to a low simmer. A lid is placed on the pan and the food is left to cook slowly.

A stew may also be cooked in the oven, when it is usually referred to as a casserole.

Health and safety

Place large stews on stovetops carefully to avoid splashes and spills. When you lift the lid from a pan, lift it away from you to avoid burning yourself on the steam.

Searing, browning and refreshing

Meat dishes may require the meat to be sealed first. This can be done to various degrees:

- browning or searing with colour – the meat is placed in hot fat or oil to seal and colour the meat.
- searing without colour – the meat or chicken is placed in moderately hot fat or oil to start to cook the surface of the meat.
- blanching and refreshing – the meat is placed in cold water and brought to the boil; it is then refreshed in cold running water.

Thickening

Most stews should have a thickened consistency. This consistency can come from a few different methods.

- Unpassed ingredients (that is, those not strained out) can cause thickening. For example, in an Irish stew all of the vegetables are left in the stew and help to make it the right consistency – you should not need to add anything else to thicken an Irish stew.
- Flour can be added to the sauce. For example, for brown lamb stew (navarin) you will cook the meat and the mirepoix (chopped carrot and onion), then you will remove the mirepoix and mix flour with the meat, browning the flour before adding the cooking liquid.
- In fricassées (white stews), the cooking liquid is thickened using a roux (a flour and butter mixture).
- Egg yolks and cream can also be used to thicken white stews, such as in a blanquette.

Stews should not be over-thickened and the sauce should stay light. Make sure you use the correct amount of thickening agent and adjust the consistency during cooking if necessary by adding more liquid or more thickening agent.

Professional tip

Do not overcook stews as this causes too much liquid to evaporate. The food also breaks up, loses its colour and spoils the flavour.

Associated techniques

There are a number of techniques associated with stewing that help the chef to prepare the dish correctly:

- **skimming** – removing scum or impurities that appear as foam or froth on the surface of the cooking liquid; stir gently from the centre with a ladle to move impurities to the edge of the pan, collect them with the edge of the ladle and place them into a bowl to be discarded
- **reduction** – with some dishes the liquid is strained and then reduced by boiling; the liquid will then be used as the base for a sauce to accompany the dish
- **straining** – removing food from the cooking liquid and draining.

Braising

Braising is a moist-heat method used for cooking larger pieces of food. The food is only half covered with liquid and can be cooked on the stovetop or in the oven. The food is cooked very slowly in a pan with a tightly fitted lid, using very low temperatures. A combination of steaming and stewing cooks the food.

Food is usually cooked in very large pieces and carved before serving. This process helps to retain the maximum flavour. It will also change the texture to make the food more tender – braising breaks down the tissue fibres in certain foods, which softens them and makes them more edible. This means that tougher, less-expensive cuts of meat and poultry can be used.

Foods that can be braised

The following foods can be braised successfully:

- meat
- poultry
- vegetables
- rice.

Liquids used for braising foods

These are the same as for stewing foods.

Temperature and time control

When braising food, the temperature should be controlled so that the liquid is barely simmering. The length of time required to cook individual dishes will depend on the item being braised, its size, shape and the type of food. For example, if lamb shanks are cooked too quickly the meat can detach from the bone before it is tender enough for the customer to enjoy.

The following is a guide to braising correctly:

- Cook the food slowly – the liquid must barely simmer.
- Use a tight-fitting lid to reduce evaporation and maintain the temperature.

- The time needed for braising will vary according to the quality of the food; cheaper cuts will need braising for longer.
- The ideal oven temperature for braising is 160 °C.

Methods

There are two methods of braising:

- **Brown braising** is used, for example, for joints and portion-sized cuts of meat. Meat must be sealed and browned first (use the same method as given for stewing). The sealed and browned meat is then placed over browned vegetables (mirepoix). The liquid is added, which is brown stock, possibly with wine or tomatoes. During the cooking process, the vegetables prevent the meat from touching the base of the pan. If it does come into contact with the pan, the meat may become tough and dry.
- **White braising** is used, for example, for vegetables. First blanch the vegetables (putting them briefly into boiling water), and then place them in a braising pan with mirepox and white stock. Add the liquid to the braising pan so that it half covers the food being braised. Once you have added the liquid, place a heavy, tight-fitting lid on the cooking pan. The lid keeps the moisture in the pan and around the food, and creates steam. This prevents the food from becoming dry and tough.

Health and safety

- Use heavy oven cloths whenever you remove the pot from the oven or lift the lid.
- When you lift the lid from the pan, lift it away from you to avoid burning yourself on the steam.
- The contents can become extremely hot, so take great care to prevent splashing when you stir them.

Once food has been braised the liquid is normally strained from the food. For foods other than vegetables this is then usually made into a sauce by reducing or thickening.

Braising

When braising a joint of meat to be served whole, remove the lid three-quarters of the way through cooking and baste the joint frequently to glaze it – this makes it look attractive when it is served.

Equipment for stewing and braising

Saucepans, sauté pans and, where large numbers of portions are being cooked, bratt pans are all considered to be traditional types of equipment for stewing and braising. These should be clean and in good repair, with no loose handles and with correctly fitting lids.

Casserole dishes are usually deep, round, ovenproof dishes with handles and a tight-fitting lid. They can be made of glass, metal (cast iron), ceramic or any other heatproof material. They are available in various sizes, some of which are then used to serve the food at the table. Always make sure you use the appropriate size and type of dish for the food that you are cooking.

Quality points for stewing and braising

To ensure the quality of finished dishes:

- Select products that are fresh, have a good appearance and smell, and are at the correct temperature.
- Trim, shape and size ingredients according to dish requirements.
- Ensure that the correct temperature, time and amount of liquid are used as this will impact on the flavour, colour, texture and taste of the dish.
- Ensure, when finishing the dish, that it has the correct consistency, appearance and portion size, and that seasoning and a garnish are added if required.

Activity

1 Briefly describe the process for the following methods of cooking:
   a stewing
   b braising.
2 What is the purpose of stewing?
3 List three types of stew.
4 List five safety points that chefs should consider when cooking by stewing or braising.
5 Name four foods that can be cooked by braising.
6 Name three types of food that could be stewed.
7 Name two pieces of equipment that are traditionally used for stewing and braising.

Baking

Baking is cooking food with dry heat in an oven. Although the food is cooked in a dry oven, steam from the food itself is part in this method of cookery.

Baking

Foods that can be baked

The following foods can be baked successfully:

- flour-based products (both sweet and savoury), which may contain meat, fish or fruit
- milk- and egg-based products
- fruit
- vegetables
- pre-prepared products (such as lasagne).

Points to consider when baking

- Temperature control is essential. Always preheat ovens to the required temperature before putting the food in; otherwise the product will be spoiled.
- Most products contain water and, once heated, this will create moisture or humidity in the oven.
- The time required will vary according to the type and quantity of foods to be baked. As a guide, larger items, such as loaves of bread, will need longer than smaller ones, such as bread rolls.
- You need to think about shelf position. In general-purpose ovens, the top part of the oven is the hottest. In convection ovens, the temperature is the same in all parts of the oven, so you can place the shelves anywhere.
- Bakery is a science, so be very accurate in your weighing and measuring.
- Avoid opening oven doors whenever possible as it will let some of the heat out. To check on the cooking, look through the glass door. Opening the oven door too quickly may adversely affect the presentation of products such as Yorkshire puddings and soufflés.
- Use oven space effectively.

Health and safety

Do not open oven doors too quickly as there is likely to be a lot of steam and hot air, which may burn your face.
Use thick, dry oven cloths when removing trays from the oven.

Methods

There are three methods of baking:

- **Dry baking** – this is done in a dry oven. The water that is naturally found in food turns to steam when it is heated. This steam combines with the dry heat of the oven to cook the food. This method is used for cakes, pastry and baked jacket potatoes.
- **Baking with increased humidity** – certain foods, such as bread, need to be baked with increased humidity. To do this, place a bowl of water in the oven or inject steam into the oven (there will be a switch on the oven to do this). The humidity of the air (the moisture in it) is increased, which in turn increases the water content of the food, keeping it moist and good to eat.
- **Baking with modified heat** – foods such as baked egg custards require the heat in the oven to be modified (reduced). To do this, place the food in a bain-marie (a tray of water). This makes the food cook more slowly and means that it does not overheat. In the case of egg custard, it also means that the egg mixture is less likely to boil, which affects the texture.

Roasting

Roasting is cooking in dry heat, in an oven or on a spit, with the aid of fat or oil. The initial heat of the oven seals the food. This prevents too many of the natural juices from escaping. Once the food is lightly browned, the oven temperature (or the temperature of the heat source when spit roasting) should be reduced to cook the inside of the food without hardening the surface.

Foods that can be roasted

The following foods can be roasted successfully:

- meats such as beef, pork and lamb
- poultry, including chicken and turkey
- vegetables.

Points to consider when roasting foods

- Always preheat ovens to the required cooking temperature. Follow the oven temperature given in the recipe.
- Adjust the shelf position according to the instructions given in the recipe. In general-purpose ovens, the top part of the oven is the hottest; in convection ovens, the temperature is the same in all parts of the oven.

- The cooking time will be affected by the shape, size, type, bone proportion and quantity of the food you are cooking.
- Meat thermometers or probes can be inserted to determine the exact temperature in the centre of the joint (the core temperature).

Methods

There are two main methods of roasting food:

1 **Roasting on a spit** – place prepared meat or poultry on a rotating spit, over or in front of fierce radiated heat.
2 **Roasting in an oven** – place whole joints and large pieces of meat and fish on a trivet. This will prevent the base of the product burning or overcooking. A trivet can consist of chopped vegetables (a bit like braising, but larger than mirepoix), or can be made up from the bones or skeleton of the product you are roasting.

> **Professional tip**
>
> With spit roasting you can see exactly how the cooking is progressing and you have easy access to the food.

Health and safety

- Take care when removing a joint of meat from the oven. It may have released a lot of fat that could cause burns or scalds. Always use thick, dry oven cloths.
- Try to avoid splashing hot fat when basting the product.

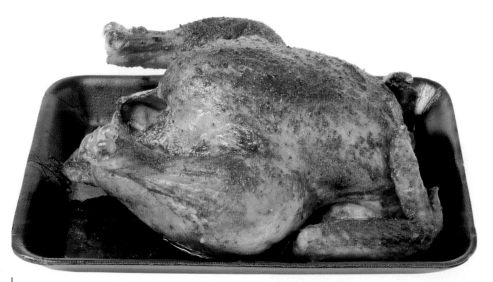

Roasting

Grilling

This is a fast method of cooking using radiant heat. The heat source transfers heat directly towards the food being grilled. Grilled food will often be slightly charred by the bars of the grill, adding colour and giving food a distinctive appearance, which adds to the presentation. Grilling is often considered to be the best cooking method for reducing fat and retaining nutrients because the food is cooked so quickly and the fat runs off the food. Barbeques are a very common type of grill, used particularly in the summer.

> **Professional tip**
>
> When grilling you have good control of the cooking process because the food is visible and accessible while it is being grilled.

Foods that can be grilled

The following foods can be grilled successfully:

- meat, such as beef, pork and lamb
- poultry, such as chicken and turkey
- vegetables
- fish.

Points to consider when grilling

- Do not grill foods for too long; cooking the food slowly will dry it out.
- Smaller, thinner items should be cooked very quickly.
- The amount of time the food is grilled for should be determined by the degree of cooking required – rare and medium cooking takes less time than well-cooked foods.
- Seal and colour food on the hot part of the grill, then move to a cooler part to complete cooking.
- Basting of food and oiling of bars will help to prevent the food from drying out and sticking to the grill.
- The position of the shelf or grill above or below the heat will influence the amount of time the item takes to cook.

Grilling

Method

Grilled foods can be cooked over heat (charcoal, barbecues, gas- or electric-heated grills/griddles), under heat (gas or electric salamanders, over-heated grills) or between heat (electrically heated grill bars or plates).

1 **Grilling over heat** – preheat grill bars and brush with oil prior to use, otherwise food will stick to them. The bars should char the food on both sides to give the distinctive appearance and flavour of grilling. When using solid fuel, allow the flames and smoke to die down before placing food on the bars, otherwise the food will be tainted and spoiled. You can marinate certain foods (such as skewered kebabs and chicken) before cooking. You can brush other foods (such as pork spare ribs) liberally with a barbecue sauce on both sides before and during cooking.

2 **Grilling under heat/salamander** – preheat salamanders and grease the bars. Steaks, chops and items that are likely to slip between the grill bars of an under-heated grill may be cooked under a salamander.

3 **Grilling between heat** – this is grilling between electrically heated grill bars or plates; it is used for small cuts of meat.

Health and safety

- When reaching over to turn food at the back of a grill, be careful of the heat coming up from underneath, which may burn your forearm. Always wear a long-sleeved jacket.
- If meat or fish has been marinated in an oil marinade, ensure that it is well drained before you place it on the grill. Food with too much oil on it may be a fire hazard if it is moved directly from the marinating container to the grill.

Equipment used for baking, roasting and grilling

There are a number of pieces of equipment that are used for baking, roasting and grilling:

- **ovens** – general purpose, convection and combination
- **grills** – under-fired or traditional grills, salamander, infra-red and contact grills
- **small equipment** – tongs, probes, slices, palette knives and skewers.

More information on these types of equipment is provided in Chapter 5.

Health and safety

Always use the correct equipment to turn and lift food on to a grill. Use tongs to turn and lift cutlets and steaks; use fish slices to turn and lift tomatoes, mushrooms and whole or cut fish.

Quality points

To ensure the quality of finished dishes there are a number of things that the chef can do during the process:

- Select products that are fresh, have a good appearance and smell, and are at the appropriate temperature.
- Prepare foods according to dish requirements: trim, shape and size as required.
- Ensure that the correct temperature, time and amount of liquid are used. These will have an impact on flavour, colour, texture and taste of the dish.
- When finishing the final dish, ensure consistency of appearance and portion size; add any seasoning and garnish if required.

Deep frying

Deep frying is the process by which small, tender pieces of food are totally immersed in hot fat or oil, and cooked quickly. The heat of the oil penetrates the food and cooks it. Although oils and lards are 'wet', deep frying is classified as a dry method of cookery. This is because it has a drying effect on the food. Often the items will be coated (usually with milk or egg and flour or breadcrumbs) before being cooked, which prevents the food from becoming greasy. Deep-fried foods can be cooked quickly and handled easily for service.

Deep frying

Foods that can be deep fried

The following foods can be deep fried successfully:

- meat, such as beef, lamb, pork
- poultry, such as chicken and turkey
- vegetables
- fish
- fruit
- flour-based products (sweet and savoury).

Fish and chips are probably the most popular kind of fried food in the UK.

Oils and fats used for deep frying

Often a mix of vegetable oils is used:

- sunflower oil
- corn oil
- rapeseed oil
- olive oil.

Most businesses do not use fats for deep frying.

Points to consider when deep frying

- Never overfill fryers with fat or oil, or with the food to be cooked.

> **Health and safety**
>
> Hot oil can cause serious burns, through either spills or accidents. Deep frying can be a very dangerous method of cooking, especially if people are not correctly trained. Only trained people should use deep fryers.
>
> Commercial deep fryers have built-in safety features, such as thermostatic controls and oil-level indicators. These safety features make commercial fryers preferable to pots on stoves.

- When deep frying it is essential to maintain the oil at the right temperature. The normal frying temperature is between 175°C and 195°C. A slight heat haze will rise from the oil when it reaches this temperature. When using free-standing fryers without a thermometer, never allow the oil to get so hot that smoke rises from it. This will give the food a bad taste and smell, and is a fire hazard. The quickest way to cool hot oil is to add fresh cold oil.

> **Health and safety**
>
> Monitor the temperature – if it is too high, the oil may easily ignite and cause a fire. Never allow oil to heat up so much that it starts to smoke. Smoke means that the hot oil could burst into flames and is very dangerous.

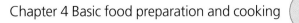

- Timing is important too. If you are cooking thicker pieces of food, you should lower the temperature. This allows the food to cook thoroughly on the inside without burning on the outside. The reverse is also true – the smaller the pieces of food, the hotter the frying temperature needs to be and the shorter the cooking time.
- Ensure that food to be fried is dry.
- After removing a batch of food, allow the oil to heat up again before adding the next batch. The temperature of the oil must be allowed to recover before the next batch is cooked. If not, the food will look pale and unappetising, and will be soggy to eat.
- Ensure that you are using the right amount of oil for the amount of food you are cooking. Too much food in too little oil will reduce the temperature drastically and spoil the food.
- Do not fry the food too far in advance of serving it – fried foods soon lose their crispness.
- Strain oil after use to remove any food particles. If these are left in the oil they will burn when the oil is next heated, spoiling the appearance and flavour of the food.
- Always cover oil when not in use to prevent the air from making it rancid.

Health and safety

Do not move a deep fryer that is either on or still hot. Avoid sudden movements around deep fryers, as they may be bumped or items may be dropped into the hot oil.

Methods

To deep fry:

1 Preheat the oil.
2 Coat the food as required (see recipe).
3 Once it has reached the required temperature, place the food carefully into the oil.
4 Fry the food until it is cooked and golden brown.
5 Drain the food well before serving.

Health and safety

- Always keep a close eye on a deep fryer and never leave it unattended.
- Stand back when placing food into the fryer to avoid steam and splash burns. Avoid putting your face, arms or hands over the deep fryer. Always wear a long-sleeved chef's jacket.

Partially cooking food before deep frying is known as blanching. The food is partly cooked (usually by boiling) in advance of service and then finished by deep frying to order. This works particularly well with certain types of potato, giving chips a floury texture inside and a crisp exterior. Preparing in advance and cooking later helps during a busy service and saves time.

Associated products

Sauces and garnishes are normally indicated in recipes; these can include tartare sauce, deep-fried parsley and lemon with fish and other fried dishes.

Shallow frying

Shallow frying is cooking food in a small quantity of preheated fat or oil in a shallow pan (a frying pan or a sauté pan) or on a flat surface (a griddle plate). As the food is in direct contact with the oil, it cooks rapidly. The high temperature used in shallow frying seals the surface of the food almost instantly and prevents the natural juices from escaping.

Shallow frying

Foods that can be shallow fried

The following foods can be shallow fried successfully:

- meat, such as beef, lamb and pork
- poultry, such as chicken and turkey
- vegetables
- fish
- eggs
- fruit
- flour-based products (sweet and savoury).

Oils and fats used

These can include the same oils that are used for deep frying, plus butter and lard.

If shallow-fried food needs to be cooked in butter, you should use **clarified butter**, which has a higher burning point than **unclarified butter**, so it will not burn as easily. Clarified butter is butter that has been melted and skimmed; after that the fat element of the butter is then carefully poured off, leaving the milky residue behind.

> ### Professional tip
>
> Some of the frying medium (oil or butter) will be absorbed by the food, which will change its nutritional content (in other words, it will make it more oily). Protect items from absorbing the oil in which they are cooked by applying a coating.

Points to consider when shallow frying

- When shallow frying continuously over a busy period, prepare and cook the food in a systematic way.
- Cleaning the pans after every use, even in batch cooking, will ensure the best presentation.
- Food should be dry to ensure that it fries correctly and that oil/fat is not spat out of the pan towards the chef.
- Food items should be placed presentation-side down first so that turning once will help enhance presentation of the finished dish.

> ### Health and safety
>
> Add food to the pan carefully, holding it away from you, to avoid being splashed by hot oil. Always keep your sleeves rolled down to prevent splashing oil from burning your forearm.

- Temperature and time control are particularly important, as all shallow-fried foods should have an appetising golden-brown colour on both sides. The temperature should initially be hot; the heat should then be reduced and the food turned when necessary.

Methods

There are four methods of shallow frying:
- **To shallow fry** (meunière), cook the food in a small amount of oil or fat in a frying pan or sauté pan. Fry the presentation side of the food first (the side that will be seen when it is on the plate). The side that is fried first will have the better appearance because the oil is clean. Then turn the food to cook and colour the other side.

- **To sauté** (toss or jump) tender cuts of meat and poultry, cook them in a sauté pan or frying pan in the same way as for shallow frying. Once the food is cooked on both sides, remove it from the pan, discard the oil and deglaze the pan with stock or wine. This liquid is then used to make the sauce to go with the food. Food such as potatoes, onions and kidneys can also be sautéed. Cut them into slices or pieces and toss them in hot, shallow oil in a frying pan until golden brown and cooked.
- **To griddle** foods such as hamburgers, sausages and sliced onions, place them on a lightly oiled, preheated griddle (a solid metal plate). Turn them frequently during cooking. Pancakes can also be cooked this way but should be turned only once.
- **Stir fry** vegetables, strips of fish, meat and poultry in a wok or frying pan by fast-frying them in a little fat or oil.

> **Professional tip**
>
> Select the correct type and size of pan. If it is too small, the food will not brown evenly and may break up. If it is too large, the areas of the pan not covered by food will burn and spoil the flavour of the food.

Associated products
Sauces and garnishes are normally indicated in recipes and may include a jus-lié with escalopes of meat, or lemon with other fried dishes.

Equipment used for deep and shallow frying
In most kitchens there will be a variety of large and small pieces of equipment used for frying, depending on the style of cooking and dishes served:
- deep fryer, thermostatically controlled, usually with a cool zone at the bottom
- shallow frying pans, sauté pans and bratt pans (for large quantities)
- specialist fryers or pans, woks, omelette pans and griddle plates.

Quality points
To ensure the quality of finished deep- and shallow-fried dishes there are a number of things that a chef can do during the process:
- Select products that are fresh, have the correct appearance and smell, and are at the appropriate temperature.
- Prepare items correctly: trim, shape and size according to dish requirements, and correctly prepare the coating to be used.
- Follow the appropriate cooking process: cook at the correct temperature, for the correct amount of time and use the correct amount of oil; this will impact on the flavour, colour, texture and taste of the dish.

■ Finish the final dish so that it is consistent, has a good appearance and appropriate portion size. Season and garnish if required, and ensure the cleanliness of service equipment.

Activity

1 Briefly describe the processes for the following methods of cooking:
   a deep frying
   b shallow frying.
2 List three types of coating that could be applied to fish before frying.
3 List five safety points a chef should consider when cooking by deep frying.
4 What are the traditional accompaniments to the following fried dishes:
   a deep-fried cod?
   b pan-fried fillet of plaice?
5 List five oils that can be used for frying foods.
6 Name three types of food that could be deep fried.
7 Briefly describe the term 'blanching' in relation to deep-fried potato dishes.
8 Describe how you would griddle sausages.
9 Why should you use clarified butter when deep frying?
10 List three pieces of equipment you could use when deep or shallow frying.

Microwave cooking

A microwave oven, which is often shortened to microwave, heats food by bombarding it with electromagnetic radiation. This causes the molecules in the food to rotate and build up heat, which cooks the food. These ovens heat foods quickly and efficiently; food is more evenly heated throughout (except in thick, dense objects) than generally occurs in other cooking techniques. This cooking process does not brown the food, so some microwaves have extra elements to brown the food to make it more attractive.

A microwave oven

Foods that can be cooked in a microwave

The following foods can be cooked in a microwave successfully:

- meat
- fish
- poultry
- egg-based products
- vegetables.

The best results are obtained when the food is of a uniform thickness and has a high water content.

Points to consider when using a microwave

- Arrange the food carefully, with the thickest parts towards the outside.
- Use glass, ceramic or plastic containers for the food – never use metal unless the manufacturer says it is safe to do so (metal containers cause sparking, which damages the oven).
- Cover foods with lids or microwave cling film while cooking, to retain moisture and reduce splashes.
- The time required will vary according to the type and quantity of foods to be cooked. Always start with the minimum time recommended and add more time as needed.
- Turn the food over or stir it at least once during cooking.
- After the cooking time has finished, remove the food from the microwave and allow it to stand for the food to finish cooking.
- Always check that the food has reached the correct temperature by using a probe.

Cold food

Preparing and serving cold food

Cold foods are popular and can be served at any mealtime, at any time of the year. Cold food can be prepared in advance and stored. This means a business can serve a large number of people in a short space of time.

Before, during and after being assembled, the foods must be kept in a cool place or refrigerator to minimise the risk of food contamination and growth of bacteria. High standards of hygiene must be maintained with all cold work. This includes personal hygiene as well as food and equipment hygiene.

Quality points when preparing cold food

- **Freshness** – foods should be bought frequently, stored correctly (usually in refrigerators below 5°C) and checked carefully to ensure that they are in good condition (with no blemishes) and within the use-by date.
- **Smell** – the smell should always be fresh and appetising.
- **Preparation** – dishes should always be prepared according to recipes and specifications, cut into even-sized portions and trimmed if necessary, with minimum waste.
- **Portions** – portion sizes will vary according to the type of establishment and the types of customers you are serving. For example, office workers generally require smaller portions than workers who are involved in manual work.
- **Appearance** – dishes should be neatly dressed and simply garnished.

Presentation of cold food

It is important that cold food is presented well so that it is attractive and appealing to customers. Remember, people eat with their eyes. The type of equipment used will depend on the style of service. Food may be served on plates or platters, or in bowls or service dishes. It is usually served straight from the display cabinet. If it is to be displayed for a long time, then a chilled display cabinet is required.

A variety of attractive containers are available for a takeaway service; all food must be clearly labelled and dated, and, if possible, nutritional content displayed.

> **Professional tip**
>
> Use a variety of fresh herbs to enhance the flavour of traditional salads and cold dishes, such as basil, tarragon, coriander, rosemary, chives and parsley.

Food safety and quality control for cold food presentation

- At all times maintain the highest standard of food hygiene when preparing and serving cold food. Separate the raw and cooked items to avoid cross-contamination.
- All equipment and utensils must be kept clean and in good condition to prevent contamination of food.

- Food for cold presentation must be of the best quality and, if cooked, must be prepared and cooked correctly following the recipe and temperature requirements precisely. Allow to cool and serve. Do not reheat any cooked food as this is a dangerous practice.
- All food items must be stored in a clean, tidy refrigerator; they must be covered, labelled and dated.
- Remember, it is a legal requirement under the Food Safety Act that high-risk food served at an ambient temperature is served within 4 hours ('ambient' means room temperature). High-risk food not served after this time may be unsafe and, therefore, should be thrown away and must not be offered to customers or staff.

Salads

Salads may be made from a wide variety of foods – raw or cooked. They may be served as an accompaniment to hot and cold foods or as dishes in their own right. Salads can be divided in two types:

- simple, using one main ingredient (for example, tomato, cucumber, green salad or potato salad)
- mixed or composite, using more than one ingredient (for example, coleslaw, Russian, mixed, Waldorf).

A rice or pasta salad can be a simple salad if it is just seasoned; it becomes a composite salad when mixed with other ingredients, such as diced peppers, sweetcorn, peas, tomatoes or diced cucumber.

Accompaniments (dressings and sauces)

Accompaniments and dressings enhance cold food dishes; they add flavour and improve the overall eating quality.

- A good vinaigrette will improve many salad items. A number of different herbs may be added to the vinaigrette.
- Different spices can be used to make the cold dishes more interesting (see Recipe 6).
- Mayonnaise can be used as an accompaniment or as a dressing (see Recipe 7).
- Crème fraiche may be used in place of yoghurt.
- In some salads sour cream is used.

Commercial mayonnaises and vinaigrettes are available, which can save time in the kitchen, and these have quite a long shelf life.

> **Professional tip**
>
> Always finish salads at the last minute, especially when using vinaigrette, so that they remain crisp and fresh.

Sandwiches

Sandwiches are a quick, timesaving snack and are widely available. The traditional sandwich is made by spreading butter or margarine on two slices of bread, placing a filling on one slice and covering it with the other. The crust may or may not be removed and the sandwich then cut into two or four pieces.

Sandwiches

Types of bread

There is a wide variety of bread available (for example, white, brown, wholemeal, granary, seeded) and many bakers will bake bread according to your specification (for instance, tomato, basil, rosemary, walnut and olive) and will slice it ready for use.

Fillings

There is an almost endless variety of sandwich fillings that can be used. Single food items, such as ham, cheese or roast beef can be used; alternatively, a mix of food items can be used, such as ham and tomato, egg and cress, and chicken and lettuce.

Types of sandwiches

There are many different types of sandwiches:

- toasted sandwich
- club sandwich
- bookmaker sandwich
- double- or triple-decker sandwich
- open sandwich.

Instructions for making some of these types of sandwich are given in the Recipes section later in this chapter.

Activity

1 Name three meal occasions where cold food items can be served.
2 Describe the differences between an open, a closed and a club sandwich.
3 Name two simple salads.
4 Name two composite salads.
5 When presenting cold dishes, apart from presentation and garnish, what else needs to be considered?
6 What is the maximum time a cold buffet can be left for presentation at room temperature?

Stocks and sauces

Ingredients

	4.5 litres	10 litres
Raw, meaty bones	1 kg	2.5 kg
Water	5 litres	10.5 litres
Onion, carrot, celery, leek	400 g	1.5 kg
Bouquet garni		

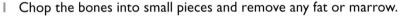

Get ready to cook

1 Chop the bones into small pieces and remove any fat or marrow.
2 Wash and peel the vegetables.
3 Prepare a bouquet garni.

Cooking

1 Place the bones in a large pot, cover with cold water and bring to the boil.
2 As soon as the water comes to the boil, take the pot to the sink and drain away the water.
3 Wash the bones and clean the pot.
4 Return the bones to the pot, cover them with the water and bring them back to the boil again.
5 Reduce the heat so that the water is simmering gently.
6 Skim the surface to remove any scum as and when required. Also wipe round the top and inside of the pot.
7 After 2 to 3 hours add the vegetables and the bouquet garni.
8 Simmer for a further 3 to 4 hours, skimming regularly.
9 When the cooking is finished, skim the stock again and strain it.

Storage suggestions

If you are going to keep the stock, cool it quickly, pour it into a suitable container and put it in the fridge. It can also be frozen.

Try something different

Chicken stock can be made in the same way using chicken carcasses and/or winglets.
- Simmer the carcasses/winglets for 1 hour, then add the vegetables and simmer for a further hour.

RECIPE 2   Béchamel (basic white sauce)

Ingredients

	1 litre	2.5 litres
Onion	0.5	1
Clove	1	1
Bay leaf	1	2
Milk	1 litre	2.5 litres
Margarine, butter or oil	100 g	400 g
Flour	100 g	400 g

Get ready to cook

Push the clove into the onion, with the sharp end going in, leaving the round end studding the outside of the onion.

Cooking

1 Add the clove-studded onion and bay leaf to the milk. Simmer, allowing it to infuse, for 5 minutes.
2 Melt the fat in a thick-bottomed pan.

3 Mix in the flour with a wooden spoon.
4 Cook for a few minutes, stirring frequently. If you are making white roux you should not allow the mixture to colour.
5 Remove the pan from the heat to allow the roux to cool.

6 Return the pan to the stove over a low heat. Gradually ladle the milk into the roux – stir the mixture back to a smooth paste each time you add a ladleful of milk.

7 Continue adding the milk, one ladleful at a time.

8 Allow the mixture to simmer gently for 30 minutes, stirring frequently.

9 Remove from the heat and pass the sauce through a conical strainer.

Storage suggestions

To prevent a skin from forming, brush the surface with melted butter. When ready to use, stir this into the sauce. Alternatively, cover the sauce with cling film.

Try something different

Béchamel is a basic white sauce that can be used as the basis for many other sauces. The suggestions below are for half a litre of béchamel, which is enough for eight to twelve portions of sauce.

Sauce	Served with	Additions per half litre
Egg	Poached or steamed fish	2 diced hard-boiled eggs
Cheese	Poached fish or vegetables	50 g grated Cheddar cheese
Onion	Roast lamb or mutton	100 g chopped onions cooked without colouring, either by boiling or sweating in fat
Parsley	Poached fish or boiled ham	1 tsp chopped parsley
Cream	Poached fish or vegetables	Add cream or natural yoghurt to give the consistency of double cream
Mustard	Grilled herrings	Add diluted English or continental mustard to give a spicy sauce

Activity

1 As a group, make all six of these sauces. Taste, discuss and assess them.
2 Suggest a variation of béchamel sauce of your own, and a dish which you might serve it with.

RECIPE 3 Velouté

Ingredients

	4 portions	10 portions
Margarine, butter or oil	100 g	400 g
Flour	100 g	400 g
Stock (chicken or fish)	1 litre	4.5 litres

This is a basic white sauce made from white stock and a blond roux.

Cooking

1 Melt the fat in a thick-bottomed pan.
2 Mix in the flour with a wooden spoon.
3 Cook out to a sandy texture over a gentle heat, allowing the lightest shade of colour (blond roux).
4 Remove the pan from the heat to allow the roux to cool.
5 Return the pan to the stove and, over a low heat, gradually add the hot stock.
6 Mix until smooth and simmering.
7 Cook for 1 hour, then pass through a fine conical strainer.

Storage suggestions

To prevent a skin from forming, brush the surface with melted butter. When ready to use, stir this into the sauce. Alternatively, cover the sauce with cling film.

Try something different

A velouté-based sauce can be used for egg, fish, chicken and mutton dishes. The suggestions below are based on half a litre of velouté.

Name of sauce	Served with	Additions per half litre
Caper	Boiled leg of mutton or lamb	2 tbsp capers
Aurora	Poached eggs, chicken	1 tsp tomato purée 60 ml cream or natural yoghurt 2–3 drops of lemon juice
Mushroom	Poached chicken	100 g sliced button mushrooms lightly cooked in a little fat or oil

Activity

Suggest an alternative velouté-based sauce of your choice. Prepare, taste, discuss and assess it.

Soup recipes

RECIPE 4 Split pea soup

Ingredients

	4 portions	10 portions
Split peas	200 g	500 g
White stock or water	1.5 litres	3.75 litres
Onion	50 g	125 g
Carrot	50 g	125 g
Bouquet garni		
Knuckle of ham or bacon (optional)		
Salt		
Stale bread	1 slice	2.5 slices
Butter or oil	50 g	125 g

Get ready to cook

1 Check and wash the peas. If pre-soaked, change the water.
2 Wash, peel and chop the onions and carrots.
3 Prepare a bouquet garni.
4 Prepare the croutons by cutting the stale bread into 1 cm cubes and then shallow frying them in the butter or oil until they are golden brown.

Any type of pulse can be made into soup, for example, split peas (yellow or green), haricot beans or lentils. Some pulses may need to be soaked overnight in cold water.

Cooking

1 Place the peas in a thick-bottomed pan.
2 Add the stock or water. Bring to the boil and skim.
3 Add the remainder of the ingredients and a little salt.
4 Simmer until tender, skimming when necessary.
5 Remove the bouquet garni and ham.
6 Liquidise the soup and pass it through a conical strainer.
7 Return the soup to a clean pan and bring it back to the boil.
8 Taste and correct the seasoning and consistency. Dilute with stock if it is too thick.
9 Serve garnished with the fried croutons.

Try something different

Add either of the following:

- a chopped fresh herb, such as parsley, chervil, tarragon, coriander or chives
- a spice or a combination of spices, such as garam masala.

Activity

Name as many types of pulse as you can (there are at least 21).

RECIPE 5   Tomato soup

Ingredients

	4 portions	10 portions
Butter, margarine or oil	50 g	125 g
Bacon trimmings (optional)	25 g	60 g
Onion and carrot	100 g of each	250 g of each
Flour	50 g	125 g
Tomato purée	100 g	250 g
Large tomatoes	2	5
Stock	1.5 litres	3.5 litres
Bouquet garni		
Salt		
Stale bread	1 slice	2.5 slices
Butter or oil	50 g	125 g

Get ready to cook

1   Peel, wash and roughly chop the vegetables.
2   Wash and chop the tomatoes.
3   Prepare a bouquet garni.
4   Prepare the croutons by cutting the stale bread into 1 cm cubes
    and then shallow frying them in the butter or oil until they are
    golden brown.

Some tomato purées can be stronger than others, so you may have to add a
little more or less when making this soup.

Cooking

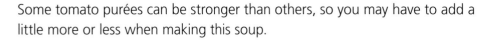

1   Melt the fat in a thick-bottomed pan.

2   Add the bacon, onions and carrots, and lightly brown these.

3   Mix in the flour and cook to a sandy texture.

4 Mix in the tomato purée, then remove the pan from the heat and allow the mixture to cool.

5 Return the pan to the heat and add the chopped tomatoes.

6 Mix well.

7 Gradually mix in the hot stock. Stir it until it is boiling.

8 Add the bouquet garni and a little salt, and simmer for 1 hour.

9 Skim the soup and remove the bouquet garni.

10 Liquidise or pass the soup firmly through a sieve, then through a medium-mesh conical strainer.

11 Return the soup to a clean pan and reheat it.

12 Taste the soup and check seasoning and consistency.

13 Serve garnished with the fried croutons.

Try something different

Try adding:
- the juice and lightly grated peel of one or two oranges
- cooked rice
- a chopped fresh herb, such as chives.

Activity

1 Name and prepare a tomato soup variation of your own.
2 Review the basic recipe for tomato soup and adjust it to meet the dietary requirements of a low-fat, vegetarian customer.

Dressings

RECIPE 6 Mayonnaise

Ingredients

	8 portions
Egg yolks, very fresh or pasteurised	3
Vinegar or lemon juice	2 tsp
Small pinch of salt	
English or continental mustard	½ tsp
Mild-flavoured oil, such as corn oil or the lightest olive oil	250 ml
Water, boiling	I tsp

It is strongly recommended that pasteurised egg yolks are used because of the risk of salmonella food poisoning.

Preparation

1 Place the egg yolks, vinegar, salt and mustard into the bowl of a food mixer.

2 Whisk until thoroughly mixed.

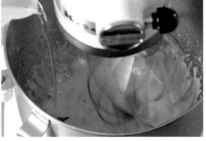

3 Continue to whisk vigorously and start to add the oil – this needs to be done slowly.

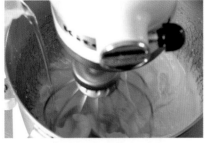

4 Keep whisking until all of the oil has been added.

5 Whisk in the boiling water.
6 Taste and correct seasoning if necessary.

Try something different

Try adding:
- fresh chopped herbs
- garlic juice – peel a clove of garlic and press it using a garlic press
- thick tomato juice.

If the mayonnaise becomes too thick while you are making it, whisk in a little water or vinegar.

Mayonnaise may separate, turn or curdle for several reasons:
- you added the oil too quickly
- the oil was too cold
- you have not whisked enough
- the egg yolks were stale and weak.

To reconstitute (bring it back together), either:
- pour 1 teaspoon of boiling water into a clean basin and gradually, but vigorously, whisk in the curdled sauce a little at a time
- whisk a fresh egg yolk with half a teaspoon of cold water in a clean basin, then gradually whisk in the curdled sauce.

Activity

1 Suggest three further mayonnaise variations.
2 Deliberately curdle some mayonnaise and reconstitute it.

RECIPE 7 **Vinaigrette**

Ingredients

	4 to 6 portions
Vinegar	2 tbsp
French mustard	1 tsp
Salt	1 tsp
Olive oil	4 tbsp

Preparation

1 Combine the vinegar with the mustard and salt.

2 Slowly whisk in the oil.

Try something different

You could use:
- English mustard in place of French mustard
- chopped fresh herbs, such as chives, parsley and tarragon
- different oils, for example sesame oil
- different vinegars, or lemon juice instead of vinegar.

Activity

Suggest two more variations to a basic vinaigrette.

Sandwiches

RECIPE 8   Toasted cheese sandwich

Ingredients

Bread	2 slices
Butter	10 g
Cheddar cheese	60 g

Toasted sandwiches can be made either by adding a filling between two slices of hot, freshly buttered toast, as described here, or by using a piece of equipment called a sandwich toaster. Some sandwich toasters will seal the sandwich, remove the crusts and cut it in half.

Cooking

1 Toast the two slices of bread.
2 Spread the toast with butter.
3 Slice the cheese and lay it on one piece of buttered toast; place the other slice of toast butter-side down on top.
4 Cut into quarters diagonally and serve.

Try something different

You can try other fillings such as banana and chocolate spread, peanut butter and jam, or add ham to the cheese sandwich.

If you are using a sandwich maker, be sure to follow the maker's instructions. They can get very hot so be careful when using them.

RECIPE 9 Club sandwich

Ingredients

Bread	3 slices
Butter	15 g
Streaky bacon	3 rashers (approx. 60 g)
Tomato	4 slices
Lettuce	3 leaves
Mayonnaise	50 ml
Cooked chicken breast	3 slices (approx. 80 g)
Eggs	2 eggs

Get ready to cook

1 Hard-boil the eggs (see Recipe 13) then peel and slice them.
2 Grill the bacon until it is crispy.
3 Wash the lettuce leaves.

Cooking

1 Toast the bread and butter it.

2 On the first slice, place slices of grilled, crispy, streaky bacon.

3 Place slices of tomato and lettuce on the bacon.

4 Put the second slice of toast on top of this and spread mayonnaise on it. Layer sliced cooked chicken breast over the top.

5 Add slices of hard-boiled egg.

6 Finally, put the third slice of toast on top. Press down carefully on the sandwich to make it as compact as possible, then secure it with cocktail sticks.

7 Cut it into halves or quarters.

Use three or four slices of bread, toasted or untoasted, to make other double-decker and triple-decker sandwiches.

Serving suggestion

Serve with potato crisps.

Salads

RECIPE 10 **Potato salad**

Ingredients

	4 portions	10 portions
Potatoes	200 g	500 g
Vinaigrette	I tbsp	2½ tbsp
Mayonnaise, natural yoghurt or crème fraiche	125 ml	300 ml
Onion or chives (optional)	10 g	25 g
Parsley or mixed fresh herbs	½ tsp	1½ tsp
Salt		

Get ready to cook

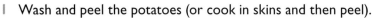

1 Wash and peel the potatoes (or cook in skins and then peel).
2 Cook potatoes by boiling or steaming.
3 Cut cooked potatoes into 0.5–1 cm dice or slices.
4 Prepare the vinaigrette (see Recipe 7).
5 If desired, blanch the onion by placing it in boiling water for 2 to 3 minutes, cooling and draining (this will reduce its harshness). Then chop it up.
6 Chop the herbs.

Preparation

1 Put the potatoes into a bowl and sprinkle on the vinaigrette.
2 Mix in the mayonnaise, yoghurt or crème fraiche and onion or chives.
3 Finally, mix in the chopped parsley or other herbs and season to taste.

Try something different

Try adding chopped mint or chopped hard-boiled egg at the end.

Activity

Suggest two or three more additions for a potato salad.

RECIPE 11 **Vegetable salad**

Ingredients

	4 portions	10 portions
Carrot	100 g	250 g
French beans	50 g	125 g
Turnip	50 g	125 g
Peas	50 g	125 g
Vinaigrette	1 tbsp	2–3 tbsp
Mayonnaise or natural yoghurt	125 ml	300 ml
Salt		

Get ready to cook

1 Peel and wash the carrots and turnips, and cut into neat dice.
2 Top and tail the beans and cut into 0.5 cm pieces.
3 Prepare the vinaigrette (see Recipe 7).

Preparation

1 Cook the carrots, beans and turnips separately in lightly salted water until tender, then refresh and drain well.
2 Cook, drain and refresh the peas. Drain well.
3 Mix all the vegetables in a basin with the vinaigrette and then mix in the mayonnaise or yoghurt.
4 Taste and correct the seasoning if necessary.

Try something different

- Potato can be used in place of turnip.
- A little of any or a mixture of the following can be chopped and added: chives, parsley, chervil, tarragon.

Activity

Suggest two or three more ingredients that could be added to a vegetable salad.

RECIPE 12 **Soused herring or mackerel**

Ingredients

	4 portions	10 portions
Herrings or mackerel	2	5
Salt and black pepper		
Button onions	25 g	60 g
Carrot	25 g	60 g
Bay leaf	0.5	1.5
Peppercorns	6	12
Thyme	1 sprig	2 sprigs
Vinegar	60 ml	150 ml

Get ready to cook

1 Clean, scale and fillet the fish.
2 Peel and wash the onion and carrots, and cut into neat, thin rings.
3 Preheat the oven to 180°C.

Cooking

1 Wash the fish fillets well and season with salt and black pepper.
2 Roll up with the skin outside and place in an earthenware dish.
3 Blanch the onions and carrots for 2 to 3 minutes.
4 Add to the fish with the remaining ingredients.
5 Cover with greaseproof paper or aluminium foil and cook in a moderate oven (180°C) for 15 to 20 minutes.
6 Allow to cool, then place in a serving dish with the onion and carrot.

This dish is also known as pickled herring.

Serving suggestion

Garnish with picked parsley, dill or chives.

Egg recipes

RECIPE 13 Boiled eggs

Ingredients

Eggs	allow one or two eggs per portion

The boiling times given in these recipes are based on the eggs being at room temperature before cooking.

Cooking soft-boiled eggs
1 Place the eggs in a saucepan, cover with cold water and bring to the boil.
2 Simmer for 2 to 2½ minutes.
3 Remove from the water and serve in egg cups.

Cooking medium-soft eggs
1 Place the eggs carefully into a pan of boiling water.
2 Bring back to the boil then simmer for 4 to 5 minutes and remove.

Cooking hard-boiled eggs
1 Place the eggs carefully into a pan of boiling water.
2 Bring back to the boil then simmer for 8 to 10 minutes.
3 Refresh until cold under running water.

RECIPE 14 **Poached eggs**

Ingredients

Eggs	allow one or two eggs per portion
Malt vinegar	1 tbsp per litre of water

Only use top-quality fresh eggs for poaching because of the large amount of thick white, which helps them to stick together in the simmering water.

Using vinegar (an acid) helps to set the egg white and also makes it more tender and white.

Cooking

1 Heat a shallow pan of water at least 8 cm deep.
2 Add one tablespoon of malt vinegar per litre of water.

3 Break the eggs into small pots.

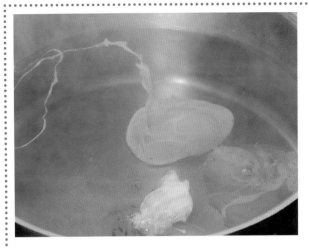

4 Carefully tip the eggs into the gently simmering water.

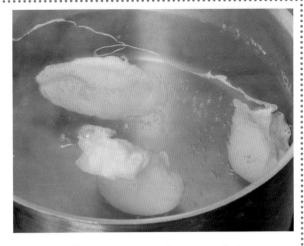

5 You will see each egg form a ball shape.

7 Remove carefully using a perforated spoon. Place into ice water to stop the cooking process, then place on a clean, dry cloth to drain off any water.

6 Cook for approximately 3 to 3½ minutes, until lightly set.

Serving suggestion

Serve on hot, buttered toast.

> **Activity**
>
> Poach two eggs: one as fresh as possible, the other stale and past its 'best before' date. Assess the results.

RECIPE 15 **Scrambled eggs**

Ingredients

	4 portions
Butter	250 g
Eggs	8
Milk (whole or skimmed)	250 ml
Parmesan cheese	12 g
Salt and black pepper	

Get ready to cook

1   Beat the eggs in a large bowl.
2   Grate the Parmesan cheese.

Cooking

1   Put the butter in a large bowl and microwave for 60 to 90 seconds, until the butter melts.
2   Mix the eggs, milk, Parmesan cheese, salt and pepper together in another large bowl.
3   Add this mixture to the melted butter.
4   Microwave the mixture on high for 2 to 3 minutes, until the eggs are set but still moist.
5   Remove from the microwave and cover. Let it stand for 2 minutes.
6   Divide the mixture into four portions and serve on warmed plates.

Serving suggestion

Serve sprinkled with freshly chopped parsley.

Rice and grain recipes

RECIPE 16 **Plain boiled rice**

Ingredients

	4 portions	10 portions
Basmati rice (dry weight)	100 g	250 g

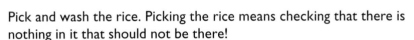

Get ready to cook

Pick and wash the rice. Picking the rice means checking that there is nothing in it that should not be there!

Cooking

1 Bring a pan of lightly salted water to the boil.
2 Stir in the washed rice and bring the water back to the boil.
3 Reduce the heat and simmer gently until tender (approximately 12 to 15 minutes).
4 Pour into a sieve and rinse well, first under cold running water then very hot water.
5 Drain off all water and leave the rice in a sieve placed over a bowl and covered with a clean tea cloth.

Health and safety

Once rice is cooked, it should be kept at a temperature above 65 °C, but for no longer than 2 hours. If it is kept at a lower temperature than this, or for longer than 2 hours, spores of a bacterium found in the soil where the rice grew may change back to bacteria and could cause food poisoning.

Avoid storing and reheating cooked rice unless it has it has been done in strict hygiene and temperature-controlled conditions.

RECIPE 17 **Braised rice (pilaff)**

Ingredients

	4 portions	10 portions
Oil, butter or margarine	50 g	125 g
Onion	25 g	60 g
Long grain rice	100 g	250 g
White stock, preferably chicken	200 ml	500 ml
Salt		

Get ready to cook

Peel the onion and chop it finely.

Cooking

1 Place half the fat into a thick-bottomed pan.
2 Add the onion and cook gently without colouring until the onion is soft (2 to 3 minutes).
3 Add the rice and stir to mix. Cook over a gentle heat without colouring for a further 2 to 3 minutes.

4 Add exactly twice the amount of stock to rice.

5 Season lightly with salt, cover with buttered greaseproof paper and bring to the boil.
6 Place in a hot oven (230–250 °C) until cooked (approximately 15 minutes).
7 When cooked, remove immediately to a cool container or pan. If the rice is left in the hot pan it will continue cooking, which will result in it overcooking and being spoilt.
8 Carefully mix in the remaining half of the fat using a two-pronged fork.
9 Taste, correct the seasoning and serve.

Try something different

- Add sliced mushrooms at the same time as the onions.
- Add freshly grated cheese (10 g to 100 g) with the fat at the end.

Activity

Cook two dishes of pilaff, one with a good, richly flavoured chicken stock, and the other with water. Taste and compare them.

Pasta recipes

RECIPE 18 Farfalle with chives and bacon

Ingredients

	4 portions	10 portions
Farfalle	400 g	1 kg
Streaky bacon	10 rashers	25 rashers
Butter or oil	50 g	125 g
Fresh chives	2 tbsp	5 tbsp
Parmesan cheese	50 g	125 g

Get ready to cook

1 Chop the chives.
2 Grate the Parmesan.

Cooking

1 Cook the pasta in lightly salted boiling water, stirring occasionally, for approximately 10 to 15 minutes (until *al dente*).
2 Meanwhile, grill the bacon until crisp, then cut it into small pieces.
3 Drain the pasta and place in a warm bowl.
4 Mix in the bacon, butter, chives and Parmesan.
5 Taste, correct the seasoning and serve.

RECIPE 19 **Macaroni pasta bake**

Ingredients

	4 portions	10 portions
Macaroni	100 g	250 g
Oil or butter (optional)	25 g	60 g
Cheddar cheese	100 g	250 g
Thin béchamel sauce	500 ml	1.25 litres
Diluted English or continental mustard powder	¼ tsp	1 tsp
Salt and black pepper		

Get ready to cook

1　Prepare the béchamel sauce (see Recipe 2).
2　Grate the cheese.
3　Dilute the mustard powder.

Cooking

1　Plunge the macaroni into a saucepan of lightly salted boiling water.
2　Boil gently, stirring occasionally, for approximately 10 to 15 minutes (until *al dente*).
3　Drain well in a colander.
4　Return to a clean dry pan and add the oil or butter.
5　Mix in half the cheese, the béchamel sauce and the mustard. Season lightly and taste to check.
6　Place in an earthenware dish and sprinkle the remaining cheese on top.
7　Brown lightly under a grill or in a hot oven.

Try something different

Add a layer of sliced tomatoes or lightly cooked sliced mushrooms to the top of the macaroni before adding the final grated cheese and browning.

Fish recipes

RECIPE 20 **Poached salmon**

Ingredients

	4 portions	10 portions
Salmon fillets (100–150 g each)	4	10
Butter or margarine	25 g	60 g
Salt		
Fish stock		Sufficient to come halfway up the fish – this will depend on the size and type of cooking vessel

Get ready to cook

1 Wash and dry the fish fillets.
2 Use the butter to grease an ovenproof dish and a sheet of greaseproof paper.

Cooking

1 Arrange the washed and dried fish fillets in the prepared ovenproof dish and season lightly.
2 Cover with the buttered greaseproof paper.
3 Add sufficient fish stock to come halfway up the fish.
4 Cook in a moderate oven at 170°C for approximately 10 minutes. The cooking time will vary according to the thickness of the fillets. Fish should *not* be overcooked.
5 When cooked, remove the fillets, drain well and keep warm and covered with greaseproof paper.
6 Strain off the cooking liquor into a small pan. Place on a hot stove and allow to reduce by half. Strain again.

Serving suggestion

Serve with a little of the cooking liquid spooned over the fish.

RECIPE 21 **Grilled fillets of sole, plaice or haddock**

Ingredients

Fillets of sole, plaice or haddock
Flour
Oil
Lemon

Get ready to cook

1 Remove the black skin from the sole or plaice. (This does not affect haddock.)
2 Wash the fish fillets and dry them well.
3 Preheat the grill. If using a salamander, grease a baking sheet.
4 Cut the lemon into slices or quarters.

Cooking

1 Pass the fillets through the flour. Shake off the surplus.
2 Brush the fillets with oil.
3 Place the fish on hot grill bars or a griddle. If the grill is a salamander, place the fish on the greased baking tray and put this under the salamander.
4 Brush the fish occasionally with oil as it cooks. Turn it carefully and grill on both sides. Do not let it overcook.

Professional tip

Oil the grill bars well, so that the fish does not stick.

Serving suggestion

Serve the fish with pieces of lemon and provide a suitable sauce, for example, salsa or a compound butter.

RECIPE 22 Baked cod with a cheese and herb crust

Ingredients

	4 portions	10 portions
Cod fillet portions (100 g each)	4	10
Fresh white breadcrumbs	100 g	250 g
Butter, margarine or oil	100 g	250 g
Cheddar cheese	100 g	250 g
Parsley	1 tbsp	2½ tbsp
Salt		
Herb mustard	1 heaped tsp	2 heaped tsp

Get ready to cook

1 Wash and thoroughly dry the fish.
2 Grate the cheese.
3 Chop the parsley.

Cooking

1 Place the fillets on a greased tray or ovenproof dish.
2 Combine all the other ingredients thoroughly. Season lightly with salt.

3 Press an even layer of the mixture on to the fish.
4 Bake in an oven at 180 °C for approximately 15 to 20 minutes until cooked. The crust should be a light golden brown.

Serving suggestion

Serve with quarters of de-pipped lemon, or a suitable sauce such as tomato or egg.

Try something different

- Add a good squeeze of lemon juice to the cod before cooking.
- Add 2 tbsp/5 tbsp milk to the cod before cooking.
- Brush with the fish with beaten egg before adding the topping.
- Cover the herb crust with slices of peeled tomato before cooking.
- Use other chopped fresh herbs, such as chives, dill or fennel, or a touch of spice, such as garam masala.

Activity

In groups, prepare, cook, taste and assess four variations of your choice.

RECIPE 23 Steamed fish with garlic and spring onion

Ingredients

	4 portions	10 portions
White fish fillets, e.g. plaice, lemon sole	400 g	1.5 kg
Salt		
Fresh ginger	1 tbsp	2½ tbsp
Spring onions	2 tbsp	5 tbsp
Light soy sauce	1 tbsp	2½ tbsp
Garlic	1 clove	2 cloves
Light oil	1 tbsp	2½ tbsp

Get ready to cook

1 Wash and dry the fish well.
2 Peel and finely chop the ginger.
3 Finely chop the spring onions.
4 Peel and thinly slice the garlic.

Cooking

1 Rub the fish lightly with salt on both sides.
2 Put the fish on to plates or dishes. Sprinkle the ginger evenly on top.

3 Put the plates into a steamer, cover tightly and steam gently until just cooked (5 to 15 minutes, according to the thickness of the fish). Do not overcook.

4 Remove the plates and sprinkle on the spring onions.

5 Brown the garlic slices in hot oil in a small frying pan.

6 Sprinkle the soy sauce and garlic slices over the fish.

Activity

Suggest two variations, then cook, serve, taste, assess and discuss them.

RECIPE 24 Grilled sardines

Ingredients

Sardines	three or four sardines per portion, depending on their size
Flour	
Light oil	

Grilling – cooking under radiant heat – is a fast method suitable for small whole fish or fillets, whole or cut into portions.

Get ready to cook

Prepare, clean, wash and thoroughly dry the fish. Fillet them if required.

Cooking

1 Pass the fish through flour (cover it in flour), shake off the surplus and place on an oiled baking sheet.
2 Brush the tops with oil and cook carefully under a hot grill, ensuring they do not burn.
3 After 2 to 3 minutes, remove the tray and turn the sardines with a palette knife. Return to the grill and cook for 2 more minutes, until lightly browned.

Serving suggestion

Serve with quarters of lemon (pips removed).

Activity

Name six other fish that could be grilled (whole or in fillets).

RECIPE 25 **Fried fish in batter**

Ingredients

	4 portions	10 portions
White fish fillets	400 g	1.5 kg
Flour		
Light oil in deep fryer		
Batter		
Flour	200 g	500 g
Salt	5 g	12 g
Eggs	1	2–3
Water or milk	250 ml	625 ml
Oil	2 tbsp	5 tbsp

Deep frying is suitable for cuts and fillets of white fish, such as cod and haddock. The fish must be coated with something that prevents the cooking oil from penetrating into the fish. This recipe uses batter.

Get ready to cook

1 Prepare, clean, wash and thoroughly dry the fish.
2 Cut the fish into 100 g portions.

Preparing the batter

1 Sift the flour and salt into a basin.
2 Make a well (a small hollow) in the flour and pour in the egg and water or milk.
3 Gradually incorporate (mix in) the flour, using a wooden spoon or whisk.

4 Beat the mixture until it is smooth.
5 Mix in the oil and allow the mixture to rest for 30 to 60 minutes before using.

Cooking

1 Pass the prepared fish through flour (cover it in flour).

2 Shake off any surplus and then pass it through the batter.

3 Taking great care, gently lower the fish, away from you, into deep oil at 175 °C.

4 Allow to cook until the fish turns a golden brown.
5 Remove carefully on to kitchen paper and allow to drain well.

Serving suggestion

Serve with either quarters of lemon (pips removed) or tartare sauce. To make tartare sauce, chop 25 g capers, 50 g gherkins and a sprig of parsley and add them to 250 ml of mayonnaise (see Recipe 6).

Try something different

Instead of batter, the fish could be coated with:
- milk and flour
- flour, beaten egg and fresh white breadcrumbs.

RECIPE 26 **Fish cakes**

Ingredients

	4 portions	10 portions
Cooked white fish and/ or salmon	200 g	500 g
Potato, mashed	200 g	500 g
Salt and pepper		
Flour	25 g	60 g
Eggs	1	2
Fresh white breadcrumbs	50 g	125 g
Light oil in deep fryer		

Get ready to cook

1   Prepare, clean, wash and thoroughly dry the fish, then poach it.
2   Prepare the mashed potato.
3   Beat the eggs.

Cooking

1   Combine the cooked fish and mashed potato. Taste and correct the seasoning.

2   Using a little flour, form the mixture into a long roll on a clean work surface.

3 Divide the mixture into two or four pieces per portion.

4 Mould each piece into a ball.

5 Pass the balls through the flour, beaten egg and breadcrumbs.

6 Using a palette knife, flatten each shape firmly. Neaten the shapes and shake off surplus crumbs.

7 Deep fry in hot oil at 185°C for 2 to 3 minutes, or until golden brown.

8 Lift out carefully and transfer to kitchen paper to drain.

Serving suggestion

Serve the fish cakes with a suitable sauce, such as tomato or tartare.

RECIPE 27 **Shallow fried fish**

Ingredients

	4 portions	10 portions
White fish fillets or small whole fish	400 g	1.5 kg
Flour		
Light oil	1 tbsp	2½ tbsp

Get ready to cook

Prepare, clean, wash and thoroughly dry the fish.

Cooking

1 Completely cover the fish with flour and shake off the surplus. (If you are using a non-stick pan, it is not essential to flour the fish.)

2 Heat the frying medium (usually a light oil) in the frying pan.

3 Shallow fry on the presentation side first.

4 Carefully turn and fry the other side.

Do not overcrowd the pan – this will cause the temperature of the oil to drop and will affect the way the fish cooks. The fish should not be overcooked but should have an appetising light golden-brown colour.

Serving suggestion

When cooked and placed on the serving plates or dishes, add:
- a slice of lemon (remove the yellow and white pith, and any pips, first)
- a sprinkling of lemon juice.

Meat recipes

RECIPE 28 **Boiled bacon**

Ingredients

Bacon joint (hock, collar or gammon joint)

Collar and hock joints usually weigh about 4.5 kg, while whole gammon joints are about 7.5 kg. You should allow for 250 g per portion.

Get ready to cook

- **Hock**: cook it whole, or bone it and tie it with string.
- **Collar**: remove the bone and tie the joint with string.
- **Gammon**: cook it whole or cut it into two or three pieces and tie it with string, if necessary.

Depending on how salty the bacon joint is, you may need to soak it in cold water for 2 to 3 hours (or longer) before cooking.

Cooking

1 Place the joint in a suitably sized pan and cover with water.
2 Bring to the boil, skim and simmer gently. The cooking time will depend on the size of the joint: simmer for approximately 25 minutes per 0.5 kg plus another 25 minutes.
3 Remove the pan from the heat and allow the joint to cool in the liquid.
4 Remove the rind, brown skin and any excess fat.

Serving suggestion

Carve into thick slices and serve with a little of the cooking liquor.

It can be accompanied by a traditional dish of puréed peas, known as pease pudding (see Recipe 48), and a suitable sauce, such as parsley or mustard.

RECIPE 29 Brown lamb or mutton stew

Ingredients

	4 portions	10 portions
Stewing lamb (shoulder, neck end, breast)	500 g	1.5 kg
Salt		
Oil	2 tbsp	5 tbsp
Onion	100 g	250 g
Carrot	100 g	250 g
Flour (white or wholemeal)	25 g	60 g
Tomato purée	1 level tbsp	2¼ level tbsp
Brown stock, mutton stock or water	500 ml	2.25 ml
Bouquet garni		
Garlic (optional)	1 clove	2–3 cloves

Get ready to cook

1 Trim the meat of any excess fat and bone, and cut into even pieces.
2 Peel and roughly chop the onion and carrot.
3 Prepare a bouquet garni.

Cooking

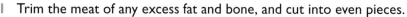

1 Season the meat lightly with salt. Heat the oil in a frying pan and fry the meat quickly until just coloured.

2 Add the onion and carrot, and continue frying until well browned.
3 Drain off any surplus fat and discard.

4 Mix in the flour with a wooden spoon and cook on a low heat, stirring continuously, for 3 to 4 minutes.

5 Mix in the tomato purée, then allow the mixture to cool slightly.

6 Put it back on the heat and gradually stir in the stock and bring it back to the boil.

7 Add the bouquet garni and garlic, if using. Skim and cover with a lid.

8 Simmer gently – in a moderate oven at 180°C or on the stove – for 1½ to 2 hours.

9 When cooked, pick out the meat and put it into a clean pan.

10 Taste and correct the sauce; pass it through a strainer on to the meat.

Serving suggestion

Serve lightly sprinkled with chopped parsley.

> **Activity**
>
> As a group, prepare, cook, serve, taste and assess the recipe using:
> 1 an ordinary brown stock
> 2 a well-flavoured lamb or mutton brown stock
> 3 water.

RECIPE 30 **Irish stew**

Ingredients

	4 portions	10 portions
Stewing lamb (shoulder, neck-end, breast)	500 g	1.5 kg
Water or white stock	400 g	1 kg
Salt		
Potatoes	100 g	250 g
Onion	100 g	250 g
Celery	100 g	250 g
Savoy cabbage	100 g	250 g
Leeks	100 g	250 g
Button onions (optional)	100 g	250 g

Get ready to cook

1 Trim the meat of any excess fat and bone and cut into even pieces.
2 Peel and wash the vegetables and cut into neat, small pieces.
3 Prepare a bouquet garni.

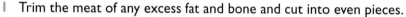

Cooking

1 Place the meat in a shallow saucepan, cover with water and bring to the boil.
2 Drain the meat under running water until meat is clean, then return it to the cleaned pan.
3 Cover with the water or white stock, season lightly with salt and add the bouquet garni.
4 Bring to the boil, skim, cover with a lid and allow to simmer for 45 minutes.
5 Add the potatoes, onion, celery, Savoy cabbage and leeks to the meat.
6 Simmer for 30 minutes, skimming frequently.
7 Add the button onions, if using, and simmer for a further 20 to 30 minutes.
8 Skim, taste and correct the seasoning.

Serving suggestion

Serve lightly sprinkled with chopped parsley. You could also accompany it with Worcester sauce and/or pickled red cabbage.

Ingredients

	4 portions	10 portions
Oil	2 tbsp	5 tbsp
Shallots	2	5
Garlic (optional)	1	2
Button mushrooms	200 g	400 g
Pork fillet	400 g	1 kg
Salt		
Chinese five spice powder	1 pinch	2 pinches
Soy sauce	1 tbsp	2 tbsp
Clear honey	2 tbsp	3 tbsp
White stock	2 tbsp	5 tbsp

Get ready to cook

1 Peel and finely chop the shallots.
2 Peel and crush the garlic.
3 Finely slice the mushrooms.
4 Cut the pork into thin strips or slices.

Cooking

1 Heat the oil in a work or frying pan
2 Add the shallots and sweat gently for 1 minute. Add the crushed garlic, if using.
3 Add the mushrooms and cook gently until softened.

4 Increase the heat and add the pork fillet strips or slices.
5 Season lightly with salt, add the Chinese five spice powder and cook for 3 to 4 minutes, tossing continuously.

6 Reduce the heat, add the soy sauce, honey, white stock and reduce for 2 to 3 minutes.
7 Taste, correct the seasoning and serve.

Serving suggestion

Serve with noodles, braised rice (see Recipe 17) or stir-fried vegetables, or a combination of these.

RECIPE 32 **Braised belly pork**

Ingredients

	4 portions	10 portions
Belly pork, boned and skinned	500 g	1¼ kg
Light oil		
Water or white stock	enough to come halfway up the meat – this will depend on the size and type of cooking vessel	
Marinade		
Fresh ginger	10 g	25 g
Red chilli	½	1
Garlic	1 clove	2 cloves
Soy sauce	15 ml	40 ml
Chinese five spice powder	½ tsp	1 tsp
Honey	1 tbsp	2 tbsp
Tomato ketchup	1 tbsp	2 tbsp
Oranges	½	1
Worcester sauce	1–2 tsp	5 tsp
Arrowroot	5 g	12 g

Get ready to cook

1 Bone and skin the pork belly, unless this has been done by the butcher. Keep the skin.
2 Finely chop the ginger and red chilli.
3 Zest and juice the oranges.
4 Mix together the ingredients for the marinade and marinate the pork overnight.

Cooking

1 Remove the pork from the marinade and drain well.
2 Sear the meat on all sides in small amount of oil in a shallow pan.
3 Place in a braising pan.
4 Add the marinade to the pan and enough water or white stock to come halfway up the meat and bring to a simmer.
5 Cover with a tight-fitting lid or foil and braise in the oven at 160°C for approx 2½ hours (or until tender).
6 Drain off the meat and allow to rest.
7 Reduce the cooking liquor or thicken it with a little arrowroot dispersed in cold water.
8 To make crackling, cut the rind (skin) into thin strips and place it on a tray. Sprinkle with salt, cover with silicone paper and another tray and bake it in oven at 190°C until crispy.

Serving suggestion

Serve with fondant potatoes and braised red cabbage.

This recipe was contributed by Iain Middleton, Team Leader for Hospitality and Catering at New College Stamford, Lincolnshire.

RECIPE 33 **Traditional braised beef**

Ingredients

	4 portions	10 portions
Lean beef (topside or thick flank)	400 g	1.25 kg
Dripping or oil	25 g	60 g
Onion	100 g	250 g
Carrot	100 g	250 g
Brown stock	500 ml	1.25 litres
Salt and black pepper		
Bouquet garni		
Tomato purée	25 g	60 g
Demi-glace or jus-lié	250 ml	625 ml

Get ready to cook

1　Preheat the oven to 160°C.
2　Wash, peel and slice the onions and carrots. Lightly fry them.
3　Trim and tie the joint.

Cooking

6　Bring to the boil, skim and cover with a lid. Cook in a moderate oven at 160°C.
7　After approximately 1½ hours' cooking, remove the meat.
8　Add the demi-glace or jus-lié, bring back to the boil, then skim and strain.

1　Season the meat and colour quickly on all sides in the hot fat to seal the joint.
2　Place the lightly fried vegetables into a small braising pan (any pan with a tight-fitting lid that may be placed in the oven) or in a casserole.
3　Place the joint in with the vegetables.

4　Add the stock – it should come two-thirds of the way up the meat – and season lightly.
5　Add the bouquet garni, tomato purée and, if available, add a few mushroom trimmings.

9 Replace the meat. Do not cover but baste frequently and continue cooking for a further 30 to 60 minutes. Braised beef should be well cooked (approximately 35 minutes per 0.5 kg plus 35 minutes). To test if it is cooked, pierce with a trussing needle – it should penetrate the meat easily and there should be no sign of blood.

10 Remove the joint and correct the colour, seasoning and consistency of the sauce.

Serving suggestion

Remove the string and carve slices across the grain. Pour some of the sauce over the slices and serve the remainder of the sauce in a sauceboat. Serve with plenty of potatoes and vegetables, or with pasta.

Professional tip

About one-third of the meat weight gives you the weight of vegetables needed.

RECIPE 34 Roast loin of pork with apple and onion sauce

Ingredients

	4 portions	10 portions
Oil		
Loin of pork on the bone	950 g	2.75 kg
Salt		
Cooking apples	2	5
Onion	1	2–3
Cider	60 ml	150 ml

Get ready to cook

1 Use a loin that is on the bone. Saw down the chine bone to make it easier to carve. The chine bone is the bone along the back of the loin that attaches the two loins together.
2 Trim off all sinew and excess fat.
3 If it has not been done by the butcher, score the skin (cut deeply with the point of a small sharp knife) in the direction that the loin will be carved. Season lightly with salt.
4 Secure it by tying a string through the chine bone.
5 Peel, core and quarter the apples, and peel and quarter the onion.
6 Preheat the oven to 200 °C.

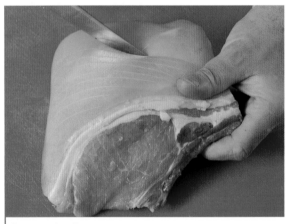

Scoring the skin

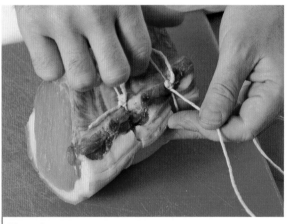

Tying the joint

Cooking

1 Heat some oil in a frying pan. Place the pork into the oil and seal it on all sides.

2 Remove the pork from the pan. Cook the apples and onions in the same pan.

3 Deglaze the pan with some of the cider.

4 Place the meat, apples and onions in a roasting tin. Add the rest of the cider and roast at 200°C for 25 minutes, then reduce the temperature to 170°C and continue to cook until done (approximately 45 minutes).

5 Remove the joint from the roasting tin and put on a plate or dish.

6 Check that it is cooked by pressing the lean meat – there should be no signs of blood in the juice.

7 Cover the joint loosely with foil and allow it to rest for 10 to 15 minutes before carving. Remove the crisp skin (crackling) and break it up.

8 Purée the apples and onions in a processor, then reheat. It should have a fairly thick consistency – if it is too thick, adjust with cider.

Serving suggestion

Slice the pork and serve with the apple and onion sauce, and gravy. A piece of the crisp skin (crackling) should be served with each portion of pork.

RECIPE 35 **Lamb kebabs**

Ingredients

	4 portions	10 portions
Lamb, lean meat	600 g	1.5 kg
Red pepper	2	5
Onion	1	3
Bay leaves	4	10
Vegetable oil	2 tbsp	5 tbsp
Dried thyme	½ tsp	1 tsp

Get ready to cook

1 Cut the meat into cubes.
2 Deseed the red pepper and cut it into squares.
3 Peel the onion and cut it into squares.

Kebabs, a dish of Turkish origin, are pieces of food impaled on skewers and cooked on or under a grill or barbecue. They are made using tender cuts of various meats with pieces of vegetables or fruits in between.

The ideal cuts of lamb to use are the lean meat of the loin or rack.

Cooking

1 Push the cubes of meat on to skewers, alternating these with squares of red pepper, onion and a bay leaf.
2 Brush with oil and lightly sprinkle with dried thyme.
3 Cook over or under a grill.

Serving suggestion

Serve with pilaff rice (see Recipe 17) and finely sliced raw onion.

Try something different

Different flavours can be added by marinating the kebabs. This involves soaking the meat, before cooking, in a combination of oil, vinegar, lemon juice, spices and herbs, for 2 hours at room temperature or 4 hours in the refrigerator.

Activity

Each member of the group should devise their own kebab from a range of ingredients: meat, vegetables, herbs and spices.

The group should then cook, serve, taste and assess each version.

RECIPE 36 **Grilled pork chops**

Ingredients

Pork chops
Salt
Oil

You can buy chops ready prepared or you can prepare them from a loin as described below.

Get ready to cook

If you are preparing chops from a loin:
- Remove the skin, excess fat and sinew.
- Cut, saw or chop through the loin in approximately 1 cm slices.
- Remove any excess bone and trim neatly.

Cooking

1 Season the chops lightly with salt.
2 Brush with oil or fat and cook on both sides on or under a moderately hot grill or salamander for approximately 10 minutes in total, until cooked through.

Serving suggestion

Garnish with a sprig of parsley and serve with hot apple sauce.

Poultry recipes

RECIPE 37 Boiled chicken with rice and suprême sauce

Ingredients

	4 portions	10 portions
Chicken		
Boiling fowl (2–2½ kg)	1	2–3
Onion	50 g	125 g
Cloves		
Carrot	50 g	125 g
Celery	50 g	125 g
Bouquet garni		
Salt		
Suprême sauce		
Butter, margarine or oil	75 g	180 g
Flour	75 g	180 g
Chicken stock	1 litre	1.5 litres
Single cream or non-dairy cream	4 tbsp	10 tbsp
Lemon juice	a few drops	a few drops
Braised rice		
Onion	50 g	125 g
Butter, margarine or oil	50 g	125 g
Long grain rice	200 g	500 g
Chicken stock	500 ml	1.25 litres

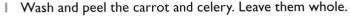

Get ready to cook

1 Wash and peel the carrot and celery. Leave them whole.
2 Peel the onions for the chicken and stud with one clove per onion.
3 Prepare a bouquet garni.
4 Peel and chop the onion for the rice.
5 Wash the chicken and truss it. Trussing is a way of tying the chicken to hold and improve its shape so that it is easier to carve.

This dish can be prepared using suprêmes (breasts) of chicken, instead of whole birds. In that case, poach the chicken in stock instead of water.

Cooking

1 Place the prepared chicken into a saucepan. Cover it with cold water. Bring to the boil and skim.
2 Add the peeled whole vegetables, bouquet garni and a little salt.
3 Simmer gently until cooked (approximately 1 to 1½ hours).
4 While the chicken is cooking, prepare the suprême sauce as per the velouté recipe (Recipe 3), and the braised rice as per Recipe 17.
5 Cook the sauce for 30 to 45 minutes.
6 Once the sauce is cooked, taste it and correct the seasoning.
7 Pass it through a fine chinois and stir in the cream.
8 To check that the chicken is cooked, insert a two-pronged fork between a drumstick and a thigh and remove the chicken from the stock. Hold it over a plate and allow the juices to come out. There should be no trace of blood in the juices. Also pierce the drumstick with a trussing needle or a skewer, which should easily slide in as far as the bone.

Serving suggestion

1 Remove the legs and cut each leg into two (drumstick and thigh).
2 Remove the breasts and cut each one in two.
3 A portion for one person is one piece of leg and one piece of breast.
4 Place the rice and chicken portions carefully on plates. The chicken can be placed on top of the rice or beside it. Coat the chicken with the sauce.

RECIPE 38 Roast chicken with herb dressing

Ingredients

	4 portions	10 portions
Chicken (1.25–1.5 kg)	1	2–3
Salt and black pepper		
Oil or butter	100 g	250 g
Onion	25 g	60 g
Parsley	1 pinch	2 pinches
Dried thyme	1 pinch	2 pinches
Breadcrumbs (white or wholemeal)	50 g	125 g
Liver from the chicken, raw (optional)		

Get ready to cook

1 Finely chop the onion.
2 Chop the parsley.
3 Chop the raw chicken liver, if using.
4 Preheat the oven to 220 °C.

Cooking

1 Lightly season the chicken inside and out with salt.
2 Place on its side in a roasting tin.
3 Cover with half of the oil or butter.
4 Place in a hot oven for 20 to 25 minutes, then turn on to the other leg.
5 Cook for a further 20 to 25 minutes, basting frequently.
6 Turn the chicken onto its back, so that the breast is upright, and roast for a further 20 to 25 minutes.
7 To test whether the chicken is fully cooked, pierce it with a fork between the drumstick and thigh, and hold it over a plate. The juice issuing from the chicken should not show any sign of blood. If using a temperature probe, insert it in the thickest part of the leg; it should read 77°C. Place the cooked chicken breast side down to retain all the cooking juices.
8 To make the dressing, gently cook the onion in the remaining oil or butter without colouring.
9 Add the herbs and breadcrumbs, and season with salt and pepper.
10 Mix in the liver.
11 Correct the seasoning and bake or steam the dressing separately, for approximately 20 minutes, until thoroughly cooked.

> **Professional tip**
>
> Arrange the chicken to cook sitting on one leg, then the other leg, and then with the breast upright, so that the whole bird cooks evenly

RECIPE 39 Poached suprême of chicken with Madeira and mushroom café cream sauce

Ingredients

	4 portions	10 portions
Butter	40 g	100 g
Shallots	40 g	100 g
Button mushrooms	160 g	400 g
Chicken suprêmes	4	10
Madeira	2 tbsp	5 tbsp
Reduced chicken stock	250 ml	625 ml
Double cream	200 ml	500 ml

Get ready to cook

1 Finely chop the shallots.
2 Slice the mushrooms.
3 Make the chicken stock.

Cooking

1 Sauté the shallots and mushrooms in butter until golden brown.
2 Divide the mushroom and shallots into equal piles in a shallow pan and place one of the trimmed chicken suprêmes on each pile.
3 Add the Madeira and bring to the boil.
4 Add the reduced chicken stock. Bring to the boil. Cover with buttered greaseproof paper.
5 Place the chicken in a oven, preheated to 170 °C, and cook for 12 minutes or until the core temperature reaches 75 °C. (In suprêmes with a wing bone, ensure that the meat near the bone reaches 82 °C.)
6 When cooked, remove the chicken from the pan and set aside.
7 Reduce the cooking liquor until it begins to thicken naturally.
8 Add the cream and reduce to a sauce consistency.
9 Season and serve with the chicken suprêmes.

RECIPE 40 **Grilled chicken breast**

Ingredients

	1 portion
Chicken breast	200 g
Salt and pepper	
Butter	25 g

Cooking

1 Season the chicken with salt and pepper.
2 Brush with oil or melted butter or margarine, and place on preheated greased grill bars, on a barbecue or on a flat baking tray under a salamander.

3 Brush frequently with melted fat during cooking; allow approximately 15 to 20 minutes each side.
4 Test if cooked by piercing with a skewer or trussing needle; there should be no sign of blood issuing from the meat.

Serving suggestion

Serve garnished with picked watercress and offer a suitable sauce separately.

Grilled chicken is also frequently served garnished with streaky bacon, tomatoes and mushrooms.

Try something different

The chicken can be marinated for 2 to 3 hours before grilling in a mixture of oil, lemon juice, spices, herbs, freshly grated ginger, finely chopped garlic, salt and pepper.

Turkey portions (breasts or boned-out lightly battered thighs) can also be grilled and marinated beforehand if wished.

RECIPE 41 Deep-fried chicken

Ingredients

Chicken pieces of your choice (boneless cuts, suprêmes)
Flour
Dried spices, e.g. paprika, Chinese five spice
Light batter
Oil in deep fryer

Get ready to cook

1 Prepare the batter (see Recipe 25 for fish in batter).
2 Mix together the flour and dried spices.
3 Heat the oil to 175 °C.

Cooking

1 Coat the chicken pieces in (pass them through) the mixture of flour and spices.
2 Then pass them through the batter.
3 Deep fry them at a temperature of 175 °C for 5 minutes.
4 When they are fully cooked, a probe in the thickest part of the chicken will read 75 °C or above and the juices will run clear.

RECIPE 42 **Sauté of chicken**

Ingredients

	4 portions	10 portions
Butter, margarine or oil	50 g	125 g
Chicken, whole (1.25–1.5 kg)	1	2–3
Salt		
Gravy	250 ml	625 ml
Fresh parsley		

If using ready-cut chicken, for four portions use two drumsticks, two thighs and two suprêmes (breasts cut in half).

Get ready to cook

1 Cut the chicken (or chickens) into pieces if you are not using ready-cut chicken.
2 Prepare the gravy.
3 Chop the parsley.

Cooking

1 Place the fat in a sauté pan over a hot stove.
2 Season the chicken pieces lightly with salt. Place them in the pan in the following order: drumsticks, thighs, breasts (you put the tougher pieces in first as they take longer to cook).
3 Cook to a golden brown on both sides. Cover with a lid.
4 Reduce the heat and cook gently until the chicken is tender.
5 Remove the chicken pieces and drain off the fat from the sauté pan.
6 Pour the hot gravy over the chicken.
7 Lightly sprinkle with chopped parsley and serve.

Try something different

You can make lots of variations to this basic recipe, such as adding:

- sliced mushrooms
- tomato concassé or tomato purée halfway through the cooking time
- freshly chopped soft herbs, such as chives, chervil or tarragon
- light spices, such as curry powder or Chinese five spice powder.

Vegetable recipes

RECIPE 43 Boiled/steamed potatoes

Ingredients

Potatoes – I kg of old potatoes will yield **4 to 6 portions**
Salt

Get ready to cook

1 Wash, peel and re-wash the potatoes.
2 Cut into evenly sized pieces, with two to three pieces per portion.

Cooking

1 Place the potatoes in a pan of lightly salted cold water and bring it to the boil.
2 Cook carefully for approximately 15 to 20 minutes.
3 Drain well and serve.

To boil potatoes or other root vegetables, just cover them with lightly salted cold water. Bring the water to the boil and cook until the vegetables are slightly firm. Do not let them go mushy. The one exception to this is potatoes that you are boiling to mash, which should be allowed to cook until they are a bit softer.

Try something different

■ Steam the potatoes rather than boiling them.
■ Brush 10 g melted butter per portion on to the potatoes.
■ Sprinkle lightly with freshly chopped parsley.

RECIPE 44 **Roast potatoes**

Ingredients

Oil or dripping for roasting
Potatoes – 1 kg of old potatoes will yield 4 to 6 portions
Salt, pinch

Get ready to cook

1 Wash, peel and re-wash the potatoes.
2 Cut into evenly sized pieces, three to four pieces per portion.
3 Dry the potatoes well.
4 Preheat the oven to 230–250°C.

Cooking

1 Heat a good measure of oil or dripping in a roasting tray.
2 Add the well-dried potatoes and lightly brown on all sides.
3 Season lightly with salt and cook for 45 minutes to 1 hour in a hot oven (230–250°C).
4 Turn the potatoes halfway through cooking.
5 Cook to a crisp, golden brown, then drain off the fat and serve.

RECIPE 45 **Chips**

Ingredients

Potatoes – 1 kg will yield 4 to 6 portions

Oil for deep frying

Get ready to cook

1 Peel and wash the potatoes.
2 Cut into slices 1 cm thick and 5 cm long.
3 Cut the slices into chips that are 5 cm long × 1 cm × 1 cm.
4 Wash well and dry in a cloth.
5 Preheat the oil in a deep oil fryer to 165 °C.

Cooking

1 Place the chips in a frying basket and slowly and carefully immerse in moderately hot deep oil (165 °C).
2 When they are almost completely cooked, drain them and place them on kitchen paper on trays until they are needed.
3 When required, raise the temperature in the fryer to 185 °C. Put the required amount of chips in a frying basket and immerse them in the deep oil.
4 Cook until crisp and golden brown.

Serving suggestion

Drain well, lightly season with salt and serve.

RECIPE 46 **Sautéed potatoes**

Ingredients

| Potatoes – 1 kg of old potatoes will yield 4 to 6 portions |
| Oil for sautéing |
| Salt, pinch |

Get ready to cook

Scrub the potatoes well (do not peel).

Cooking

1 Plain boil or steam the potatoes for approximately 15 minutes.
2 Cool them slightly and then peel them.
3 Cut them into 3 mm slices.
4 Toss the slices in hot shallow oil in a frying pan until nicely browned.
5 Season lightly with salt.

Serving suggestion

Serve sprinkled with freshly chopped parsley.

RECIPE 47 **Jacket potato**

Ingredients

Large baking potato

Olive oil

Salt and black pepper

Get ready to cook

Scrub the potato well to remove all the dirt from the skin.

Cooking

1 Rub a little olive oil on the skin of the potato and then rub in the salt and pepper.
2 Either cut a large cross on the top of the potato or prick each side with a fork to let out the steam when cooking.
3 Put the potato on a plate and microwave on full for 5 minutes.
4 Remove the potato from the oven, turn it over and cook for a further 3 minutes on full.
5 Check it is cooked by gently squeezing it. If it feels undercooked return it to the microwave and cook for a further minute.
6 Let the potato stand for 5 minutes to finish cooking.

Serving suggestion

Cut open and serve with butter or a filling.

Try something different

For a crisp outer skin, follow stages 1 to 3 and then bake the potato in a conventional oven at 200 °C for 20 minutes. This will give a traditional baked potato in half the time.

RECIPE 48 **Pease pudding**

Ingredients

	4 portions	10 portions
Dried yellow split peas	200 g	500 g
Water	500 ml	1.25 litres
Onion	50 g	125 g
Cloves		
Carrot	50 g	125 g
Bacon trimmings	50 g	125 g
Butter or margarine	50 g	125 g
Salt		

Get ready to cook

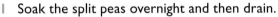

1 Soak the split peas overnight and then drain.
2 Peel the onion and then push a clove into it, sharp end first, so the round end is on the outside of the onion.
3 Preheat the oven to 180–200 °C.

Cooking

1 Place all ingredients except the butter into a thick-bottomed saucepan. Cover with a tight-fitting lid.
2 Bring to the boil and skim the water.
3 Allow the peas to cook, preferably in an oven at 180–200 °C, for 2 hours.
4 Remove the onion, carrot and bacon, and either pass the peas through a sieve or use a food processor.
6 Return the peas to a clean pan and mix in the butter. Taste and correct the consistency, which should be firm.

RECIPE 49 Boiled/steamed cauliflower

Ingredients

	4 portions	10 portions
Cauliflower	1 medium sized	2 large

All vegetables that can be boiled can also be steamed. The vegetables are prepared in the same way for boiling and steaming. To steam vegetables, place them in steamer trays and salt lightly. Steam them under pressure for as short a time as possible. The less time they are cooked for, the more nutritional value and colour they will keep.

Get ready to cook

1 Remove the outer leaves of the cauliflower.
2 Trim the stem.
3 Hollow out the stem using a potato peeler or cut into florets and wash.

Cooking

1 Place the cauliflower in lightly salted water. Bring the water to the boil.
2 Boil or steam for approximately 10 to 15 minutes if you have left the cauliflower whole, or 3 to 5 minutes if you are using florets. Do not overcook.
3 Drain well. If you have cooked it whole, cut it into four even portions before serving.

Serving suggestion

- Serve plain or lightly coated with melted butter.
- Add some cream to a Béchamel sauce (see Recipe 2) and pour it over the cauliflower.
- Place the portioned cauliflower on a tray or dish. Coat it with a cream-enriched Béchamel sauce and sprinkle with grated cheddar or Parmesan cheese. Lightly brown the topping under the salamander or in a hot oven.

RECIPE 50 **Red onion and sweetcorn frittata**

Ingredients

	4 portions	10 portions
Red onion	½ (or 1 if small)	1
Carrot	50 g	125 g
Oil	5 ml	15 ml
Ground paprika	1 pinch	2 pinches
Fresh tomatoes, ripe	2	5
Sweetcorn	20 g	50 g
Potato	100 g	250 g
Parsley	1 tsp	1½ tsp
Eggs	3	5
Milk	250 ml	625 ml
Black pepper		
Cheddar cheese	100 g	250 g

Get ready to cook

1 Peel and finely chop the onion and carrot.
2 Peel the tomatoes, then deseed and finely dice them.
3 Peel the potatoes and dice them (cut them into 1 cm cubes).
4 Cook the diced potatoes in boiling water. Drain well.
5 Chop the parsley.
6 Grate the cheese.
7 Preheat the oven to 180°C.

Cooking

1 Shallow fry the onions and carrots in the oil without colouring, then remove from the heat.
2 Sprinkle with paprika and drain off any excess oil.
3 Add the diced tomatoes, sweetcorn, potatoes and chopped parsley to the pan and combine all the ingredients.
4 Place the mixture into a suitable ovenproof dish.
5 Whisk the eggs and milk together and season with black pepper.
6 Pour the eggs and milk mixture over the vegetables in the ovenproof dish.
7 Sprinkle with Cheddar cheese.
8 Bake in the oven at 180°C for approximately 15 minutes or until the mixture has set.
9 Allow to rest slightly before cutting into portions and serving.

Serving suggestion

Serve hot or cold with salad.

RECIPE 51 Grilled vegetable bake

Ingredients

	4 portions	10 portions
Aubergine	250 g	725 g
Courgette	400 g	1 kg
Red peppers	3	8
Vegetable oil	90 ml	225 ml
Pesto	1 tbsp	2½ tbsp
Garlic cloves	2	5
Breadcrumbs	60 g	150 g
Parsley	1 tbsp	5 tbsp
Basil	1 tbsp	5 tbsp
Cheshire cheese	80 g	200 g

Get ready to cook

1 Cut the aubergine and courgettes into 5 mm slices.
2 Deseed the peppers and cut into 1 cm dice.
3 Peel and crush the garlic.
4 Chop the parsley and basil.
5 Grate the cheese.
6 Preheat the oven to 150–180 °C.

Pesto is a green sauce made from fresh basil leaves, garlic, toasted pine nuts, Parmesan cheese and olive oil. It can be bought readymade.

Cooking

1 Sprinkle the aubergine, courgette and red peppers with the oil, pesto and crushed garlic.
2 Lightly grill the vegetables on a griddle pan.
3 Line a suitable shallow dish with half of the breadcrumbs and the chopped parsley and basil.
4 Arrange the aubergines and courgettes in the dish, overlapping in rows with the peppers.
5 Mix the grated cheese into the remaining breadcrumbs and sprinkle this mixture over the vegetables.
6 Bake in a moderate oven (150–180 °C) for approximately 20 minutes.

Serving suggestion

Serve with a suitable salad, such as mixed leaves with rice noodles seasoned with soy sauce, or garnished with tomato, chopped onion and avocado.

RECIPE 52 **Courgette and pepper frittata**

Ingredients

	2 portions
Courgette	I medium
Red pepper	I medium
Fresh mixed herbs	2 tsp
Salt and black pepper	
Vegetable oil	2 tsp
Eggs	4
Cheddar cheese	25 g

Get ready to cook

1 Cut the courgette into 2 cm squares.
2 Deseed the pepper and cut into 2 cm squares.
3 Grate the cheese.
4 Chop the herbs.

Cooking

1 Put the courgette, red pepper, herbs and seasoning into a microwave dish with the vegetable oil. Cook on High for 3 minutes.
2 Beat the eggs together with two tablespoons of water.
3 Add the eggs to the other ingredients and stir. Cover and cook on High for 90 seconds.
4 Remove from the microwave, stir well and cook on High for 2 minutes.
5 Remove from the microwave and let stand for 3 minutes.
6 Scatter on the grated cheese and microwave for 1 minute.
7 Remove from the microwave, cut into squares and serve either hot or cold.

Serving suggestion

Serve hot as a light lunchtime meal.

RECIPE 53 **Vegetable casserole with herb dumplings**

Ingredients

	4 portions	10 portions
Casserole		
Vegetable oil	2 tbsp	5 tbsp
Onion	50 g	125 g
Garlic cloves	2	5
Carrot	100 g	250 g
Parsnip	100 g	250 g
Swede	100 g	250 g
Turnip	100 g	250 g
Jerusalem artichokes	60 g	150 g
Fresh thyme	1 tsp	2½ tsp
Fresh parsley	1 tsp	2½ tsp
Button mushrooms	100 g	250 g
Vegetable stock	1 litre	2.5 litres
Yeast extract, e.g. Marmite	1 tsp	2½ tsp
Ground pepper		
Dumplings		
Plain flour	200 g	500 g
Baking powder	10 g	25 g
Vegetable suet	100 g	250 g
English mustard powder	2 tsp	4 tsp
Water	60 ml	180 ml
Fresh parsley	1 tsp	2½ tsp
Fresh chervil	1 tsp	2½ tsp
Fresh tarragon	1 tsp	2½ tsp
Fresh oregano	1 tsp	2½ tsp
Fresh rosemary	1 tsp	2½ tsp
Fresh basil	1 tsp	2½ tsp

Get ready to cook

1 Peel and chop the onion.
2 Peel and crush the garlic cloves.
3 Peel the carrots, parsnip, swede, turnip and Jerusalem artichokes. Cut into 0.5 cm pieces.
4 Chop all of the fresh herbs.
5 Clean the mushrooms and cut into quarters.

Cooking

1 Shallow fry the onion, garlic, carrots, parsnips, swede, turnip and Jerusalem artichokes for 5 to 10 minutes. Stir continuously.

2 Sprinkle with the fresh thyme and parsley. Add the mushrooms and cook for a further 5 minutes.

3 Add the vegetable stock, yeast extract and season with ground pepper. Simmer until the vegetables are tender.

4 Prepare the dumplings by sifting the flour with the baking powder.

5 Mix in the shredded suet.

6 Dilute the mustard powder in half of the water. Add this, and the herbs, to the flour Mix well.

7 Add the rest of the water to the flour mixture and mix to a soft dough.

8 Knead and form into small dumplings.

9 Cook the dumplings in the casserole, or separately in vegetable stock, for 10 to 15 minutes.

Serving suggestion

Serve the casserole with the dumplings in a suitable dish.

Pastry and bread recipes

RECIPE 54 Short pastry

Ingredients

	5–8 portions	10–16 portions
Soft flour	200 g	500 g
Salt	pinch	large pinch
Lard or vegetable fat	50 g	125 g
Butter or margarine	50 g	125 g
Water	2–3 tbsp	5–8 tbsp

Short pastry is made from soft flour and fat, which gives the pastry a crumbly 'short' texture. The amount of water required can vary according to the type of flour: a very fine flour can absorb more water.

Heat (such as warm weather conditions or excess contact with hot hands) will affect the quality of the pastry.

Get ready to cook

Ensure that your hands are well scrubbed, rinsed under cold water and dried.

Preparation

1. Sieve the flour and salt into a bowl or on to a cool surface.
2. Using your fingertips, lightly rub the fat into the flour until it has a sandy texture.
3. Make a well in the centre of the mixture.
4. Add enough water to make a fairly firm paste. Mix it together, handling it as little and as lightly as possible.
5. Keep working it gently with your hands until it forms a dough.
6. Allow the pastry to rest, covered with a damp teacloth, in a cool place (refrigerator) before using. This allows the pastry to relax, which means there is less chance of it shrinking when it has been pinned out (rolled out using a rolling pin) and moulded into shape.

RECIPE 55 **Sweet pastry**

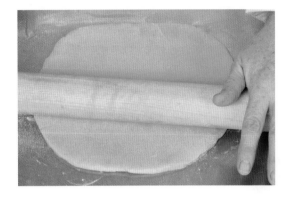

Ingredients

	4 portions	10 portions
Soft flour	200 g	500 g
Salt	pinch	large pinch
Butter or margarine	125 g	300 g
Caster sugar	50 g	125 g
Egg, medium sized	1	2–3

Preparation

1 Sieve the flour and salt, and mix in lightly.
2 Rub in the butter to achieve a sandy texture.
3 Beat the sugar and the egg together.
4 Make a well in the centre of the flour and butter mix.
5 Pour in the egg and sugar, and gently mix into the flour and butter to form a dough.
6 Allow it to rest in a cool place covered with cling film or a damp cloth.

Troubleshooting when making pastry

If your short or sweet pastry is too hard, you may have:
● added too much water
● added too little fat
● not rubbed in the fat sufficiently
● handled and rolled it too much
● over-baked it.

If your pastry is too soft and crumbly, you may have:
● added too little water
● added too much fat.

If your pastry is blistered, you may have:
● added too little water
● added the water unevenly
● rubbed in the fat unevenly.

If your pastry is soggy, you may have:
● added too much water
● had the oven too cool
● not baked it for long enough.

If your pastry is shrunken, you may have:
● handled and rolled it too much
● stretched it while handling it.

RECIPE 56 **Fruit pies**

Ingredients

	4 portions	10 portions
Fruit	400 g	1 kg
Granulated sugar	100 g	250 g
Water	2 tbsp	5 tbsp
Short pastry using flour weight of	100 g	250 g
Milk		

Bramley apples are ideal; they also combine well with blackberries, damsons and gooseberries.

Rhubarb and cherry pies also work well.

Get ready to cook

1 Make the short pastry and keep it refrigerated until you need it.
2 Prepare and wash the fruit. Remove any stalks, leaves or stones. If using apples, peel, cut into quarters, remove the core and slice.
5 Preheat the oven to 220 °C.

Cooking

1 Place the fruit in a half-litre pie dish.
2 Add the sugar and water (for an apple pie, add a clove).
3 Roll out the pastry to 0.5 cm thick to the shape of the pie dish. Use as little dusting flour as possible on the table surface, the pastry and rolling pin. Allow the pastry to relax for a few minutes.
4 Dampen the rim of the pie dish with water or milk and press a thin strip of pastry on to it.
5 Carefully roll the pastry on to the rolling pin and then unroll it over the top of the fruit, being careful not to stretch it.
6 Seal the pastry on to the dish rim firmly and cut off any extra pastry.
7 Brush the pastry with milk and sprinkle with sugar.
8 Place the pie on a baking sheet and bake it in a hot oven (220°C) for about 10 minutes.
9 Reduce the heat to 180°C and cook for a further 20 to 30 minutes (if the pastry colours too quickly, cover it with greaseproof paper or foil).

Serving suggestion

Serve with custard, cream or ice cream.

RECIPE 57 Bread rolls

Ingredients

	8 rolls	20 rolls
Strong flour	200 g	500 g
Yeast	5 g	12 g
Liquid (half water, half milk)	125 ml	300 ml
Butter or margarine	10 g	25 g
Caster sugar	¼ tsp	½ tsp
Salt	small pinch	large pinch
Egg, beaten for eggwash	1	2

Cooking

1 Sieve the flour into a bowl and warm in the oven or on the stove.
2 Cream the yeast in a basin with a quarter of the liquid.
3 Make a well in the flour and add the dissolved yeast.
4 Sprinkle over a little of the flour, cover with a cloth and leave in a warm place until the yeast ferments (bubbles).
5 Add the remainder of the warmed liquid, the fat, sugar and salt.
6 Knead firmly until smooth and free from wrinkles.
7 Return to the basin, cover with a cloth and leave in a warm place to prove (double in size).
8 Knock back (lightly knead) the dough to remove the air and bring it back to its original size.
9 Mould the dough in a roll and cut into even pieces.
10 Mould the pieces into the shapes you want. Place them on a lightly floured baking sheet and cover with a cloth.
11 Leave in a warm place to double in size.
12 Brush gently with eggwash.
13 Bake in a hot oven at 220 °C for approximately 10 minutes.
14 Remove from the oven and place the rolls on a cooling rack.

Try something different
Gently add 50 g of sultanas and 50 g of chopped walnuts at stage 8.

Fruit recipes

RECIPE 58 **Poached pears in red wine**

Ingredients

	4 portions	10 portions
Water	100 ml	250 ml
Red wine	300 ml	50 ml
Granulated sugar	125 g	300 g
Lemon zest	1	2
Cinnamon stick	1	3
Pears (firm, e.g. Williams or Comice)	4	10

Fruits are poached in flavoured liquids, that is, stock syrup or wines with the addition of spices to enhance the flavour of the fruit. The fruit can be cooked whole or in pieces, depending on how it is going to be used.

Get ready to cook

Grate the lemon zest.

Cooking

1 Place the water, wine and sugar into a saucepan and heat gently to dissolve the sugar.
2 Add the lemon zest and cinnamon stick.
3 Peel the pears neatly without removing the stalks.
4 Place the pears upright in the pan, ensuring that they are fully covered with liquor. Cover with greaseproof paper and a lid.
5 Bring to the boil and simmer until the pears are cooked. They should be tinged red and tender when pricked with a skewer.
6 The pears can be removed from the syrup to cool, or cooled quickly in the liquid to store.
7 Reduce some of the cooking liquor to make a sauce or glace to serve with the pears.

Professional tip

When peeling white fruit, such as pears and apples, you can place them into water with lemon juice to stop them from oxidising and going brown.

RECIPE 59 **Stewed fruit**

Ingredients

	4 portions	10 portions
Seasonal fruit: rhubarb, apricots, apples, plums, strawberries, pears	500 g	1.25 kg
Caster sugar	50 g (75 g for rhubarb)	125 g
Water	30 ml	75 ml

Get ready to cook

1 Prepare the fruit – peel if necessary; hull strawberries (remove the tops).
2 Chop all the fruit into even-sized pieces, discarding any stones.

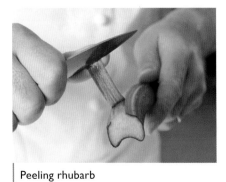

Peeling rhubarb

Hulling a strawberry

Cooking

1 Place the fruit in a pan and add the sugar.
2 Add water and cook on a medium heat with the lid on.

3 Once the fruit has softened, remove the lid and let the liquid reduce. You want to end up with a fairly thick consistency.

Professional tip

When you are stewing fruit, it is best to decide how much sugar to add by tasting the fruit. If your fruit is really ripe and sweet, you'll need less than suggested in the recipe opposite.

Serving suggestion

Serve over cereal, yoghurt, pancakes, granola or muesli. It is also great as a crumble filling. Stewed apple can be served with roast pork.

Try something different

If using rhubarb, try adding some freshly grated ginger (a 2.5 cm piece) to bring out the flavour.

RECIPE 60 Pancakes with lemon

Ingredients

	4 portions	10 portions
Plain flour	100 g	250 g
Salt	small pinch	pinch
Milk	250 ml	625 ml
Eggs	1	2–3
Butter, melted, or a light oil	10 g	25 g
Light oil for frying		
Caster sugar	50 g	125 g
Lemon	1	2

When making a batch of pancakes, keep them flat. Pile them on to a warm plate, sprinkling a little sugar in between each. Fold them when ready for service. Lightly sprinkle them again with sugar and dress nearly overlapping on service plates.

Cooking

1 Sieve the flour and salt into a basin.
2 Make a well and add the milk and egg, gradually incorporating the flour from the side of the bowl.
3 Beat vigorously with a wooden spoon or whisk to a smooth batter. This should be thick enough to just coat the back of a spoon.
4 Mix in the melted oil.
5 Heat the pancake pan and clean it thoroughly.
6 Add sufficient oil to just thinly coat the pan. Heat this until it begins to smoke.
7 Add just enough pancake batter to thinly coat the pan.
8 Cook for a few seconds until brown.
9 Turn over and cook the second side for half the time.
10 Turn on to a warm plate, sprinkle with sugar, fold in half then fold again. Serve two pancakes per portion with a quarter of lemon (remove the pips).

Try something different

If a thicker pancake is required, add another 20 g to 60 g of flour to the recipe.
Use orange segments in place of lemon.
Spread the pancakes lightly with warmed jam and roll them up.

Chapter 5   Introduction to healthy eating

Learning objectives

By the end of the chapter you should:
- Know the effects of food on the body
- Know the different food groups and their contribution to a healthy, balanced diet

Why the body needs food

Our bodies need fuel to work properly, in the same way that a car needs fuel to make it work. If you put petrol into a diesel car it will not work and, similarly, we must make sure we put the right fuel into our bodies to help them work properly.

Nutrients in foods help our bodies to do everyday things such as moving, growing and seeing. They also help our bodies to heal themselves if they are injured, and a balanced diet can help to prevent illness and disease.

Benefits of a healthy diet

Putting the right mixture of fuel in our bodies will help our bodies to work properly. This is often called eating a **balanced diet**. If we also have a reasonable amount of exercise we can expect the following benefits.

Increased energy levels for both work and leisure

The food we eat gives us energy. Energy is measured in **calories**. An average man needs around 2,500 calories a day to maintain his weight. For an average woman, that figure is around 2,000 calories a day. The amount of energy you need will depend on:
- your age – growing children and teenagers may need more energy

- your lifestyle – if you do manual labour you may need more calories
- your size – your height and weight can affect how quickly you use energy (larger people need more energy).

If you have the correct energy levels you will feel better at work, not get tired so quickly, and be able to enjoy time away from work much more.

Maintaining a healthy weight

To maintain a healthy weight, you need to balance the amount of calories you consume through food and drink with the amount of calories you burn through physical activity.

To lose weight in a healthy way, you need to use more energy than you consume by eating a healthy, balanced diet with fewer calories, or by increasing your physical activity.

The correct body mass index

To work out your body mass index (BMI) you need to know your height in metres and your weight in kilograms.

Multiply your height in metres by itself and then divide your weight by this number. For example, if you are 1.6 metres tall and weigh 56 kg:

1.6 metres × 1.6 metres = 2.56

56 ÷ 2.56 = 21.875

If your answer comes out at 25 or less, then you have a healthy BMI. If it is more than 25, you are likely to be overweight and should seek medical advice about losing weight.

Increased life expectancy

People who do not eat healthily will normally die much younger than people who do eat healthily. A poor diet can reduce your life expectancy by 20 years or more.

Reduced risk of heart attacks, diabetes, cancer and stroke

All of these conditions can be the result of being overweight, and many of these cannot be cured once you have them.

> **Activity**
>
> State the benefits of a healthy diet.

> **Key words**
>
> **Nutrient** – a chemical providing nourishment and purpose in the diet.
>
> **Balanced diet** – eating the right amounts of carbohydrates, fats, proteins, vitamins, minerals and fibre to ensure good health. Food should also provide the appropriate amount of energy and adequate amounts of water.
>
> **Calories** – the units used to measure how much energy food contains.

Major food groups

The main nutrient groups are:

- carbohydrates
- proteins
- fats
- vitamins
- minerals
- water.

Carbohydrates

Carbohydrates provide most of the energy that our bodies need. There are three sub-groups of carbohydrate: sugars, starches and fibre.

Foods high in carbohydrates

Sugars

Sugars are the simplest form of carbohydrate. There are several types of sugar:

- **glucose** – found in the blood of animals and in fruit and honey; when meat is grilled or fried the glucose helps it to go brown
- **fructose** – found in fruit, honey and cane sugar
- **sucrose** – found in beet and cane sugar; this is the main type of sugar used in cooking and for sweetening your tea
- **lactose** – found in milk
- **maltose** – found in cereal grains and used in beer making.

Starches

Our bodies have to digest starch and turn it into sugar to get the energy from it. We cannot digest raw starch very well, which is why many of these items are cooked before eating, especially those made from grains. Starches are found in the following foods:

- pasta
- cereals
- cakes, biscuits and bread
- wholegrains, such as rice, barley and tapioca
- powdered grains, such as flour, cornflour, ground rice and arrowroot
- vegetables, particularly potatoes, peas, pumpkins and sweetcorn
- unripe fruit, such as bananas, apples and pears; when they are ripe the starch has been changed into sugar, which makes them sweeter.

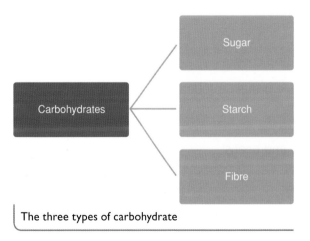

The three types of carbohydrate

Fibre

Unlike other carbohydrates, dietary fibre cannot be digested and does not provide energy for the body. However, it is essential for a balanced diet because it:

- helps to remove waste and toxins from the body, and maintains bowel action
- helps to control the digestion and processing of nutrients
- adds bulk to the diet, helping us to stop feeling hungry; it is used in many slimming foods.

Fibre is found in:

- fruit and vegetables
- wholemeal and granary bread
- wholegrain cereals
- wholemeal pasta
- wholegrain rice
- pulses (peas and beans) and lentils.

Proteins

We need protein so that our bodies can grow and repair themselves. Babies and children require more protein in their diet than adults do, as it helps them to grow. The lifespan of the cells in our bodies varies from a week to a few months. As cells die they need to be replaced.

Protein is also needed to help us carry out the normal functions of living, which are controlled by proteins called **enzymes** and **hormones**.

We can also use protein for energy. Any protein that is not used up in repairing and growing cells is converted into carbohydrate or fat, and stored by the body.

Animal protein is found in:

- meat
- game
- poultry
- fish
- eggs
- milk and cheese.

Vegetable protein is found in:

- seeds
- pulses
- peas and beans
- nuts
- wheat
- special vegetarian products such as Quorn, which is made from a fungus.

Foods high in protein

Fats

Fats are naturally present in many foods and are an essential part of our diet.

- Fats provide the body with energy.
- Fats form an insulating layer under the skin; this helps protect the vital organs and keep the body warm.
- Fat is also needed to build cell membranes in the body.
- Fats are found in a number of foods including meat, fish, vegetables, cereals, seeds and nuts.

Vitamins

Vitamins are chemicals that are vital for life. They are found in small amounts in many foods. If your diet is deficient in vitamins you can become ill or unhealthy. Vitamins help with many of our bodily functions, such as growth and protection from disease.

Table 5.1 shows the most important vitamins, how they are used in the body and what foods they can be found in.

Foods rich in vitamins

Table 5.1 Important vitamins

Vitamin	How it is used in the body	Ingredients containing it
Vitamin A	Helps children to grow Helps the body resist infection Helps with vision	Fatty foods Dark green vegetables Eggs
Vitamin B	Helps convert carbohydrates into energy Helps children to grow Good for the nervous system	Yeast Liver and kidney Oats
Vitamin C	Helps cuts to heal Helps children to grow Prevents gum infections	Fruit Green vegetables Potatoes
Vitamin D	Controls how the body uses calcium Essential for healthy bones and teeth	Oily fish Dairy produce Egg yolks

Minerals

There are 19 minerals in total, most of which our bodies need in very small quantities to function properly.

- We need minerals to build our bones and teeth.
- Minerals help us to carry out bodily functions.
- Minerals help to control the levels of fluids in our bodies.

The most important minerals for our bodies are given in Table 5.2.

Table 5.2 Important minerals

Mineral	How it is used in the body	Ingredients containing it
Calcium	Builds bones and teeth Helps muscles to work Helps blood to clot	Milk Green vegetables Wholemeal bread
Iodine	Helps the thyroid gland to work (affecting growth and weight)	Seafood
Iron	Helps keep blood healthy	Lean red meat and offal Wholemeal flour Fish
Phosphorus	Builds bones and teeth Good for the brain	Cheese Eggs Fish
Potassium	Regulates water in the body Helps muscles and nerves to work	Leafy vegetables Citrus fruit Bananas
Sodium	Regulates water in the body Helps muscles and nerves to work	Salt

Water

Water is vital for life. We cannot survive for very long without it. We lose water from our bodies through urine and sweat, and we need to replace it regularly to prevent dehydration. It is recommended that we drink about 1.2 litres (2 pints) a day. This should be drunk at regular intervals.

Our organs need water to function properly:

- Water regulates our body temperature – when we sweat the water evaporates from our skin and cools us down.
- Water helps to remove waste products from our bodies – if these waste products are not removed they can release poisons, which can damage our organs or make us ill.
- We need water to help our bodies absorb nutrients, vitamins and minerals, and to help our digestive system.
- Water acts as a lubricant, helping our eyes and joints to work and stay healthy.

Water is vital to life – you should drink 1.2 litres (2 pints) every day

Sources of water are drinks of all kinds as well as foods such as fruits, vegetables, meat, eggs and fibre.

Professional tip

Always offer water in a restaurant. Tap water is more environmentally friendly than bottled water.

Activity

1 List four types of ingredients that contribute to a healthy diet.
2 What is the purpose of fibre in the diet?
3 What valuable nutrient is contained in oily fish?

Tips for a healthy, balanced diet

The fuel we need is made up of the different nutrients described above. We need to have the right mixture of these in our diet. The Food Standards Agency (FSA) suggests the balance of food that will give you the right mixture.

The eatwell plate

FOOD
STANDARDS
AGENCY
food.gov.uk

Use the eatwell plate to help you get the balance right. It shows how much of what you eat should come from each food group.

The Eatwell plate provides guidance on a balanced diet

It is important to remember that it is the *balance* in your diet which is important, and that chocolate, sweets and chips can all be part of a balanced diet.

Professional tip

There are no bad foods, just bad diets that have an imbalance of nutrients.

The food pyramid can help you to choose a healthy diet by showing you what you can eat more of and what you should eat less of. You should eat more of the foods at the bottom of the pyramid, and less of the foods in the smaller section at the top of the pyramid.

The food pyramid helps you to select a healthy diet

The best way to stay fit and healthy is to eat a diet high in fruit, vegetables, wholegrains and plant-based foods such as beans and lentils, but low in fat, sugar and salt. This will ensure that you receive all of the nutrients detailed above in the correct quantities.

Nutritionists from the NHS give very simple advice on eating a healthy diet:

1 Base your meals on starchy foods and choose, where possible, wholegrain items or jacket potatoes.
2 Eat a variety of fruit and vegetables. While the government recommends five portions a day there is no medical evidence to prove that this improves health or reduces your risk of cancer. However, fruit and vegetables do give you fibre, which is important to your health.
3 Eat fish at least twice a week and eat oily fish, which is rich in omega 3 oils, once a week.
4 Cut down on saturated fats and sugar.
5 Eat less salt (a maximum of 6 g a day).
6 Be active and exercise regularly.

7 Don't get thirsty – drink at least 1.2 litres (2 pints) of water or other non-alcoholic drinks a day.

8 Don't skip breakfast.

Eat a variety of fruit and vegetables

Salt in your diet

Salt is an important preservative and has been used for thousands of years to prevent food from going off. Salt also brings out the flavour of foods, which is why it is used in cooking.

However, too much salt in your diet can raise your blood pressure, which puts you at increased risk of health problems such as heart disease and stroke. High blood pressure often has no symptoms but, if you have it, you are more likely to develop heart disease or have a stroke.

Adults should eat no more than 6 g of salt a day – that's around one full teaspoon. Children should eat less.

You don't have to add salt to food to be eating too much – 75 per cent of the salt we eat is already in everyday foods such as bread, breakfast cereal and ready meals.

A healthy, balanced diet has low levels of salt

The following foods are almost always high in salt due to the way they are made and you should eat them less often or have smaller amounts to cut down on the amount of salt in your diet:

- bacon
- cheese
- ham
- salami
- salted and dry roasted nuts
- smoked meat and fish.

Other foods that might be high in salt are bread products such as crumpets, bagels and ciabatta, crisps, pizza, breakfast cereals and many ready meals and sauces.

Avoid adding salt when cooking food, especially to dishes that already contain salty ingredients.

To see how much salt is in food you buy, read the labels on the food.

Groups of people needing different diets

There are various reasons why people may follow a particular type of diet. This could be because they have special nutritional needs, or for religious or cultural reasons.

Pregnant and breast-feeding women

Pregnant and breast-feeding women should avoid foods that have a high risk of food poisoning, such as soft, mould-ripened cheese, raw eggs, undercooked meat, poultry and fish. They should also avoid alcohol.

Expectant mothers require a well-balanced, nutritious diet that is high in vitamins and minerals, including folic acid and vitamin B9, which are found in leafy green vegetables such as spinach, orange juice and enriched grains. Folic acid reduces the risk of a baby being born with a serious neural tube defect such as spinal bifida. They should not, however, increase vitamin A in their diet, as too much could harm the baby, so they should avoid liver and pâté.

Breast-feeding women need high levels of nutrition to support the baby and their own well-being.

This young child has special dietary needs, and so does her pregnant mother

People who are ill

People who are ill, at home or in hospital, need balanced meals with plenty of nutrients to help them recover. Good nutritious food is part of the healing process. Their food should also be easy to eat and digest.

People who want to lose weight

Weight-loss diets should only be started after taking medical advice. Most weight-loss diets will be either low fat or low calorie, or a mixture of both. All foods have calories, so eating less food will reduce the calorie intake. As part of these diets doctors usually recommend more exercise, which helps to use up the calories in the food as well as the calories stored in the body.

People who are ill need plenty of nutrients

Always seek medical advice before starting a weight-loss diet

Vegetarians

Most vegetarians – people who do not eat meat – choose to eat this way because they believe it is healthier, or because they do not agree with eating animals, rather than for a medical reason. They avoid foods that would cause an animal to be killed.

Vegetarians have a lower risk of heart disease, stroke, diabetes, gallstones, kidney stones and colon cancer than people who do eat meat. They are also less likely to be overweight or have raised cholesterol levels.

Vegans
Vegans do not eat dairy products, eggs, or any other animal product.

Cultural/religious diets

Different cultures and religions often have their own ways of cooking and different types of cuisine. Our culture and/or religion may affect what we choose to eat and our taste preferences.

People who follow some religions do not consume, or are forbidden from consuming, certain foods and drinks; others restrict foods and drinks during their holy days. Some religions associate dietary and food preparation practices with rituals of their faith. For example:

- Christians celebrate Christmas, Shrove Tuesday and Easter with special foods. Some Christians fast during Lent.
- Muslims are only permitted to eat meat from a Halal butcher and they fast during Ramadan.
- About half of all Hindus are vegetarian and do not eat meat.
- Sikhs do not have strict rules about food but many are vegetarian.
- Buddhists are vegetarians.
- Jews have strict dietary laws. Shellfish, pork and birds of prey are forbidden. Jews may only eat meat purchased from a Kosher butcher.

Diabetics

Insulin is the chemical hormone that controls the level of sugar in the blood. **Diabetes** is a condition where a person cannot produce insulin, does not produce energy from the insulin the body produces, or the insulin produced does not work. There are a large number of people in our society with diabetes and it is on the increase due to the high levels of sugar in our diet and an increase in obesity. Diabetes can be fatal if not treated.

Diabetes is on the increase due to high levels of sugar in our diet

Each diabetic will have different dietary requirements; therefore, there is no one diabetic diet that will work for everyone. People should pick a diet that matches their individual needs.

Key words

Diabetes – a medical condition where the body cannot regulate glucose levels in the body.

Finding the balance between the amount of carbohydrates and fat is important. It is necessary for diabetics to cut down on the amount of fat, particularly saturated (animal) fat, and instead choose monounsaturated fats, such as olive oil and rapeseed oil. Diabetics should eat regular meals based on starchy carbohydrate foods such as bread, pasta, chapattis, potatoes, yam, noodles, rice and cereals. They should also include plenty of fresh fruit and vegetables in their diet.

Activity

1 What is the difference between a vegetarian and a vegan diet?
2 What are the two most common types of weight-loss diets?
3 For a chosen religion, describe how religious beliefs have an effect on the diet.
4 List reasons why you think diabetes is on the increase.

Allergies and intolerances

Food allergies

The term **food allergy** is used to describe a rapid and potentially serious response to a food by your immune system. Eating food that you are allergic to can trigger symptoms such as a rash, wheezing and itching; allergic reactions can be fatal.

The most common food allergies among adults are to nuts – usually peanuts, walnuts, hazelnuts and brazil nuts – fish and shellfish. Children often have allergies to dairy products such as milk and eggs, as well as to peanuts, other nuts and fish.

People who suffer from an allergy normally carry an EpiPen, which contains adrenaline to counteract the effect of an anaphylactic shock (a severe allergic reaction that may include breathing difficulties). The person injects themselves with the pen as soon as they realise they have eaten the food to which they are allergic.

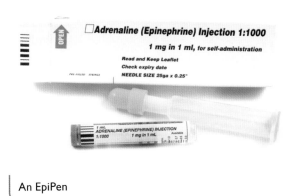

An EpiPen

Food intolerances

Food intolerances are more common than food allergies. The symptoms tend to come on more slowly – often hours after eating the problem food – and typically include stomach cramps and bloating.

It is possible to be intolerant to a number of different foods, which can make it hard to identify what foods are causing the problem. One of the most common is **lactose intolerance**, which means the person will be affected by foods with lactose in them (milk and all products made with milk).

One person in 100 suffers from **coeliac disease**, which is when the person has an adverse reaction to **gluten**. This is the protein found in flour and other grains. However, coeliac disease is not an allergy or an intolerance to gluten. It is a condition in which the person's immune system mistakes substances found inside gluten as a threat to the body and attacks them. The results of this can be diarrhoea, bloating and weight loss.

Activity

1　What is the difference between a food allergy and a food intolerance?
2　If you were lactose intolerant, what ingredients would you need to look out for on food labels?

Food labelling

Most pre-packed food items have labels that give nutritional information. This is limited to some of the major nutrients and does not cover all of them. The labels focus on those that have most affect on a healthy diet. Reading them can help you to plan a balanced diet.

The labels usually include information on:

- energy – in kilojoules (kj) or kilocalories (kcal), usually referred to as calories
- protein
- carbohydrates – including starch, sugar and fibre
- fat – usually split between saturated and unsaturated fat
- sugars (if not shown as part of the carbohydrates)
- salt or sodium.

This nutritional information is provided per 100 g and sometimes per portion of the food.

Key words

Food allergy – when the body has an immediate adverse reaction to certain types of food; it can be fatal.

Food intolerance – when the body reacts adversely to certain types of food, but it does not involve the immune system and produces less dramatic symptoms than an allergy.

Lactose intolerance – a person with lactose intolerance will be adversely affected by foods with lactose in them, such as milk and all products made with milk.

Coeliac disease – a person with coeliac disease will have an adverse reaction to gluten.

Gluten – the protein found in flour and other grains.

Food labels often include colours to indicate if the food is high in each of these ingredients (a traffic light system):

- red means high
- amber means medium
- green means low.

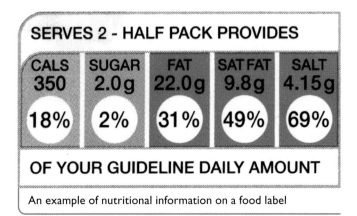

SERVES 2 - HALF PACK PROVIDES

CALS	SUGAR	FAT	SAT FAT	SALT
350	2.0 g	22.0 g	9.8 g	4.15 g
18%	2%	31%	49%	69%

OF YOUR GUIDELINE DAILY AMOUNT

An example of nutritional information on a food label

Total fat

- high (red): more than 17.5 g of fat per 100 g
- medium (amber) 3 g to 17.5 g of fat per 100 g
- low (green): 3 g of fat or less per 100 g.

Saturated fat

- high: more than 5 g of saturated fat per 100 g
- medium 1.5 g to 5 g of saturated fat per 100 g
- low: 1.5 g of saturated fat or less per 100 g.

Sugars

- high: more than 22.5 g of total sugars per 100 g
- medium 5 g to 22.5 g of total sugars per 100 g
- low: 5 g of total sugars or less per 100 g.

Salt

- high: more than 1.5 g of salt per 100 g (or 0.6 g sodium)
- low: 0.3g of salt or less per 100 g (or 0.1g sodium).

Salt is also called sodium chloride and, sometimes, food labels only give the figure for sodium. There is a simple way to work out how much salt you are eating from the sodium figure:

salt = sodium × 2.5

So a figure of 2 g sodium is 5 g of salt.

Some labels show the percentage of each food compared with **reference intake (RI)**. RI is an estimate as to how many kilocalories, fat, saturated fats, sugars and salt an average person needs – this figure has largely superseded 'recommended daily allowance' (RDA); RDA was seen as a target, whereas RI shows the maximum amount that should be consumed.

RI gives the following guideline figures (based on an average woman):

- energy: 8,400 kJ/2,000 kcal
- total fat: 70 g
- saturates: 20 g
- sugars: 90 g
- salt: 6 g

Activity

1 Using food labels to help you, compare two different loaves of bread and explain which one is the most healthy.
2 How would you recommend cooking green beans to minimise the loss of nutrients? Explain your answer.

Stretch yourself

1 Write down all you ate and drank yesterday.
2 Using information from the *Manual of Nutrition*, calculate how much of each of the following you consumed:
    - total calories
    - total fat
    - saturated fat
    - sugar
    - salt.
3 Compare this with the RI and see if you had a balanced diet.
4 Suggest ways that you could make your diet more balanced by changing some of the less healthy items for more healthy ones.

Stretch yourself

1 Collect menus from local restaurants (you may be able to find these online) and estimate the nutrient content of their main course dishes.
2 See if you can find menus with nutritional information on them and compare them with your estimates. How well did you do?

Chapter 6 — Introduction to food commodities

Chapter 6

Introduction to food commodities

Learning objectives

By the end of this chapter you will:
- Know the main food commodities
- Know where the main food commodities can be obtained
- Know how the main food commodities should be stored

This chapter will look at each of the main food commodities. It will describe them, state where they may be obtained and describe how to store them.

Information on how to prepare and cook these commodities can be found in Chapter 4.

What are the main types of food commodity?

Commodities are the ingredients that are bought by the business to be turned into meals.

The main commodities covered in this chapter are:
- meat
- poultry
- fish
- dairy
- fruit and vegetables
- pasta, grains (including rice), beans and pulses
- convenience foods.

Activity

Write down all the places you, or your family, buy food from to take home and cook.

Key words

Commodities – ingredients that can be bought to be turned into meals.

Meat

Beef

Beef is a red meat and comes from cattle that are bred for beef, such as Aberdeen Angus and Devon Ruby Red. Other cattle are bred for dairy products and do not produce such good quality beef.

Quality points

- The lean meat should be bright red and marbled with small flecks of white fat. The fat should be creamy-white, firm and brittle.
- A carcass of beef weighs about 360 kg; it is then butchered into the main joints as shown below.

A cow

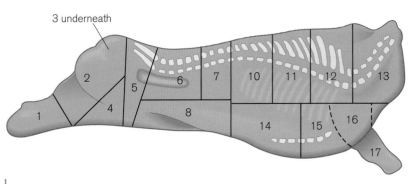

How a carcass of beef is divided into joints

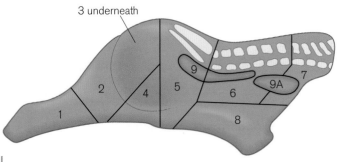

The hindquarter (rear half) of the carcass in more detail

The joints shown in the diagrams are:

1 shin
2 topside
3 silverside
4 thick flank
5 rump
6 sirloin
7 wing ribs
8 thin flank
9 fillet

9A fat and kidney
10 fore rib
11 middle rib
12 chuck rib
13 sticking piece
14 plate
15 brisket
16 'leg of mutton' cut
17 shank.

Common cuts of beef

Table 6.1 show the most common cuts of beef, their typical uses and a guide to how expensive they are.

Table 6.1 Common cuts of beef

Cut of beef	Uses	Price guide per kg
Fillet steak	Grilling, frying, roasting	£££££
Sirloin steak	Grilling, frying, roasting	££££
Rump steak	Grilling, frying, roasting	£££
Fore rib	Roasting	££
Topside	Roasting	££
Brisket	Slow roast	£
Flank	Braising, stewing	£
Skirt	Mince	£

The more expensive cuts of beef can be cooked quickly and eaten very rare or undercooked. The cheaper cuts need a longer cooking time to tenderise the meat and make them edible.

> **Professional tip**
>
> Remember that Aberdeen Angus and Hereford are breeds of cattle and do not indicate that the beef is either Scottish or English. Always check the origin of the beef.

Veal

Veal comes from calves (young beef cattle) that are less than 8 months old. These are normally the male calves of dairy cattle, which are of no use to dairy farmers. Because the calf is young, the meat is much paler than beef and is classified as a white meat.

A veal calf

Quality points

- The lean meat should be pale pink in colour and firm in texture. The fat should be firm and pinkish white.
- A carcass of veal from a 6- to 7-month-old calf weighs about 150 kg.

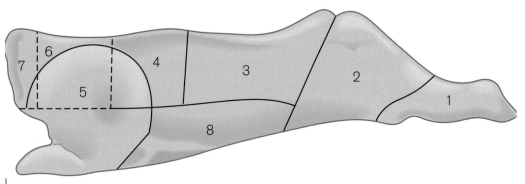

How a veal calf is cut into joints

The joints shown in the diagram are:
1 the knuckle
2 the leg
3 the loin
4 the best end
5 the shoulder
6 the neck end
7 the scrag
8 the breast.

Common cuts of veal

Table 6.2 show the most common cuts of veal, their typical uses and a guide to how expensive they are.

Table 6.2 Common cuts of veal

Cut of veal	Uses	Price guide per kg
Fillet steak	Grilling, frying, roasting	£££££
Escalope	Grilling, frying	££££
Chump steaks	Grilling, frying	£££
Chops	Grilling, frying	£££
Shoulder	Roasting	£££
Breast	Rolled and roasted	££
Mince		££
Shin (osso buco)	Stewing	££

Veal is a premium product and is generally a bit more expensive than beef. In the past there were concerns over animal welfare, but UK veal is now produced under very humane conditions.

> **Professional tip**
>
> Always check that veal is from the UK, which has the highest welfare standards for veal production.

Lamb

Lamb is meat from sheep that are less than a year old. Meat from sheep that are over a year old is called mutton.

A lamb (a young sheep)

Quality points

■ The lean meat should be reddish-pink in colour and have a firm, fine texture. The fat should be bright white, hard, brittle and flaky.

■ A carcass of lamb weighs about 16 kg.

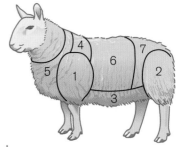

Joints of lamb and their position on the body

The joints shown on the diagram are:

1 the shoulder
2 the leg
3 the breast
4 the middle neck
5 the scrag end
6 the best end (or rack)
7 the saddle.

Common cuts of lamb

Table 6.3 show the most common cuts of lamb, their typical uses and a guide to how expensive they are.

Table 6.3 Common cuts of lamb

Cut of lamb	Uses	Price guide per kg
Cutlet	Grilling, frying, roasting	£££
Leg (including leg steaks)	Grilling, frying, roasting	£££
Fillet	Grilling, frying	££
Shoulder	Roasting	££
Diced	Stewing	££
Mince		£
Belly	Boned and rolled for slow roast	£

English or Welsh lamb is a premium product and is more expensive than New Zealand lamb.

Pork

Pork is meat from pigs and, in recent years, it has become common to name the breeds used, such as Berkshire, Gloucester Old Spot or Tamworth. Pigs are also used to make bacon, and pork is the most common type of meat in sausages. Most pigs are slaughtered at about 7 months old if they are going to be used for pork, and at about 9 months if they are going to be used for bacon.

A pig

Quality points

- The lean meat should be pale pink in colour and have a firm texture. The fat should be firm, white and smooth.
- A pig carcass for pork weighs about 40 kg, and for bacon about 60 kg.

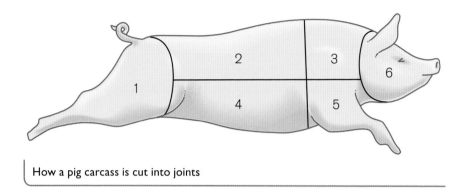

How a pig carcass is cut into joints

The joints shown in the diagram are:
1 the leg
2 the loin
3 spare rib
4 the belly
5 the shoulder
6 the head.

Common cuts of pork

Table 6.4 show the most common cuts of pork, their typical uses and a guide to how expensive they are.

Table 6.4 Common cuts of pork

Cut of pork	Uses	Price guide per kg
Fillet	Grilling, frying, roasting	££
Boneless leg	Roasting	££
Loin chops	Grilling, frying	££
Boneless shoulder	Rolled and roasted	£
Mince		£
Diced	Stewing, pork pies	£

As can be seen from this table, pork is cheaper than beef or lamb, making it one of the more economical meats.

Buying meat

A whole carcass of meat will be cheapest per kilogram, but very few businesses will be able to use all the cuts in a carcass, which can lead to wastage.

Most caterers purchase their meat from a wholesale catering butcher, who will be able to cut and joint the meat to the exact requirements of

the business. They will deliver daily and usually offer the widest choice and range of food. Many of these butchers source their meat from local suppliers.

When ordering meat, caterers should always specify exactly what **grade** of meat they require, and use the national quality grading systems for beef, lamb, veal and pork.

Some large food suppliers, such as 3663, Bookers and some local wholesalers, may also supply meat along with groceries, but it may be more expensive than a butcher and they will not carry the full range of cuts. They normally offer only the cheaper cuts.

Smaller firms may use a local butcher, who will be able to deliver, and may offer more flexibility than a wholesaler. They may be more expensive per kilogram than a wholesaler, however.

It is also possible to buy direct from the farms, which can reduce the travel costs and environmental impact; this also helps to support local employment.

All deliveries must be in a refrigerated van. All suppliers must be able to trace the meat back to the farm it came from in case of any problems with the meat.

Storing meat

- Fresh meat should be kept in a refrigerator at a temperature between 1 °C and 4 °C. It should be taken out of any bags, put into a tray to catch blood and covered. Raw meat should be stored at the bottom of the fridge, below other foodstuffs.
- Frozen meat must be stored at a temperature between –18 °C and –20 °C. It must always be fully thawed before cooking, otherwise the centre of the meat may be undercooked, and this can be a health hazard.

Activity

1   Explain why cheaper cuts of meat tend to need a slower cooking time.
2   What are the key quality points to think about when buying fresh pork?

Poultry

Poultry means birds bred for food and it includes chicken, turkey, geese and ducks. Poultry is easier to digest than meat and is normally low in fat.

Quality points
- Chickens should be firm to touch, with a flexible breast bone and with white unbroken skin. They should have a full breast and feel quite dry. Corn-fed chickens will be slightly yellow.

- Chickens used in catering vary in size from 1 kg to 3 kg and are normally used for grilling, frying and roasting. Larger chickens are generally tougher and will be boiled to make them tender.
- Turkeys are much larger and can weigh from 3.5 kg to 20 kg. They are traditionally roasted at Christmas but can make a good alternative for a family roast dinner at other times of the year.

A chicken

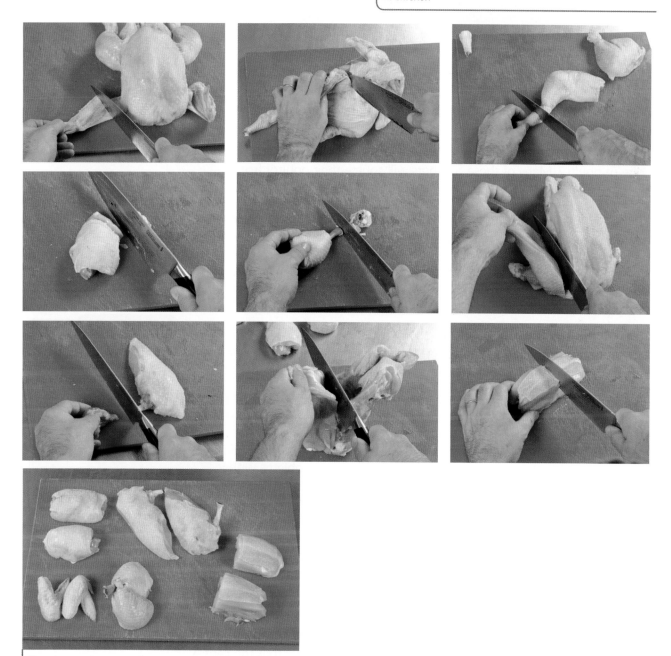

Step-by-step process of cutting up a whole chicken

A turkey

Buying poultry

Most caterers purchase their poultry from a wholesale catering butcher, who will be able to provide whole poultry as well as poultry joints, such as suprêmes. They will deliver daily and usually offer the widest choice and range of poultry. Many of these butchers will source their poultry from local suppliers.

When ordering poultry caterers should always specify exactly what size birds they want, to ensure the portion sizes are correct.

Some large food suppliers, such as 3663, Bookers and some local wholesalers, may also supply poultry, but they may be more expensive than a butcher.

Smaller firms may use a local butcher, who will be able to deliver, and may offer more flexibility than a wholesaler. They may be more expensive per kg than a wholesaler, however.

It is also possible to buy direct from farms, which can reduce the travel costs and environmental impact; this also helps to support local employment.

All deliveries must be in a refrigerated van. All suppliers must be able to trace the poultry back to the farm it came from in case of any problems with it.

Storing poultry

- Fresh poultry should be kept in a refrigerator at a temperature between 1 °C and 4 °C. It should be taken out of any bags, put into a tray to catch blood and covered. Raw poultry should always be stored at the bottom of the fridge, below other foodstuffs.
- Frozen poultry must be stored at a temperature between −18 °C and −20 °C. Chickens are potential carriers of **salmonella** and **campylobacter** and must always be fully thawed before cooking to ensure that the centre of the bird is cooked and that these **pathogens** are killed off.

Activity

Explain why fresh poultry is likely to be infected with organisms that can cause food poisoning.

Fish

Fish is a good source of protein as well as other nutrients. Due to its increasing popularity there has been an increase in the number of fish farms to meet the demand. Farmed fish is cheaper than wild fish, which can be very expensive.

There are over 200 species of edible fish, and these are split into two main categories: oily fish and white fish. Some of the more common species are shown in Table 6.5.

Table 6.5 Common species of edible fish

Oily fish	White fish
Salmon	Cod
Trout	Haddock
Tuna	Plaice
Mackerel	Dover sole
Red mullet	Monkfish
Red snapper	Shark

Quality points

Fresh fish should:

- have bright eyes
- have no missing scales
- feel moist and slippery
- be firm to touch
- give off very little smell.

Old fish smell more, have sunken eyes and missing scales.

> **Professional tip**
>
> Always trust your own sense of smell. If the fish does not smell fresh, do not use it.

Buying fish

Most caterers purchase their fish from a wholesale catering fishmonger, who will be able to supply whole fish and fish fillets, as well as shellfish. They will deliver daily and usually offer the widest choice and range of fish. They source their fish from some of the large fish markets around the UK, as well as overseas. Fish from overseas are normally flown into the UK, which can make them more expensive.

When ordering fish, caterers should always specify exactly what size fish they require, and what size fillets.

Some large food suppliers, such as 3663, Bookers, and some local wholesalers, may also supply frozen fish, but they may be more expensive than a fishmonger and will not carry as big a range.

Smaller firms may use a local fresh fishmonger, who will be able to deliver and may offer more flexibility than a wholesaler. They may be more expensive per kg than a wholesaler, however.

Some firms in fishing ports are able to buy direct from the fishermen, but the choice will be limited to what they catch and the chef will have to go to the market to buy it. Buying locally can reduce the travel costs and environmental impact, however, and also helps to support local employment.

All deliveries must be in a refrigerated van. All suppliers must be able to trace the fish back to the supplier it came from in case of any problems.

Storing fish

- Fresh fish is best stored on layers of crushed ice in a refrigerator at a temperature between 1 °C and 4 °C.
- If the fish is whole when delivered, it is best to gut it and wash it well before storage.

- As most fish have a shelf life of about 10 days from being caught, if kept properly during storage and transit, it is best to order fish fresh each day and use it within 24 to 48 hours.
- Frozen fish must be stored at a temperature between −18 °C and −20 °C. It must always be fully thawed before cooking, otherwise the centre of the fish may be undercooked, and this can be a health hazard.

Activity

1 Why is farmed salmon so much cheaper than wild salmon?
2 Which would you use for smoked salmon, and why?
3 What two things you would check for first on fresh fish, without touching the fish?

Dairy

This includes milk and milk products, such as butter, cheese, yoghurt and cream.

Milk

Most commercial milk has been **pasteurised**, a process in which milk is heated to 72 °C for 15 seconds to kill bacteria and then rapidly cooled to 3 °C. Most dairy products are made from pasteurised milk.

Milk is usually around 3.9 per cent fat, so some customers prefer to have semi-skimmed milk, which is 1.7 per cent fat, or skimmed milk, which is almost fat free. One drawback of this is that a lot of the flavour is in the fat, so reducing fat reduces the flavour. Some recipes require full-fat milk to work properly.

Key words

Pasteurise – a process in which milk (or another liquid) is rapidly heated and then cooled to kill bacteria.

Full-fat and skimmed milk

Cream

The cream that is skimmed off milk is sold as cream. Single cream is 18 per cent fat, double cream is 48 per cent fat and clotted cream is 55 per cent fat. Cream is used to add flavour and thickening to sauces.

Butter

Butter is made by churning fresh milk and is about 80 per cent fat and 20 per cent water. It is useful in cooking for frying food, and also in making a number of different pastries.

Butter

Cheese

There are thousands of different cheeses throughout the UK, and millions in the world, as an increasing number of dairy farmers make their own cheese. The cheese-making process involves **curdling** the cheese and separating the solid **curds** from the liquid **whey**. **Rennet** is added to help the cheese to set, and then other processes are used depending on whether the cheese is to be a soft cheese or a hard cheese.

Cheese

Key words

Curdling – the process of separating the solids in milk from the liquid; the solids form **curds**.

Whey – the liquid left when the solids in milk have formed into curds.

Rennet – an enzyme that helps animals to digest milk; rennet used in cheese-making is taken from the stomach of calves (although a vegetarian alternative is available).

> **Activity**
>
> Explain why cheese made from unpasteurised milk is still safe to eat.

Yoghurt

Yoghurt is made from fermented milk; its fat content depends on the type of milk it was made from. It is thicker than milk and can be used in some recipes to replace cream.

Yoghurt

Buying dairy products

Most caterers purchase milk from a dairy with daily deliveries. This could be part of a national company or a local supplier.

Butter may come from the dairy or a food wholesaler.

Cheeses may come from a wholesaler, but may be bought from a specialist cheese supplier or a local delicatessen. Some caterers purchase local cheeses directly from the manufacturers, which helps to support local employment.

All dairy deliveries must be in refrigerated vans.

Storing dairy products

- Most dairy products should be stored in a refrigerator at a temperature between 1 °C and 4 °C. UHT (long-life) products can be stored in a dry store until opened, and then should be put in a fridge.
- Cheeses continually mature and dry out. In an ideal world you would store them between 10 °C and 15 °C. Keeping them in a fridge speeds up the drying out process, so wrap them up well to stop this happening. Cheese should be taken out of the fridge prior to service to allow it to reach room temperature and develop its flavour.

Eggs

Eggs are often linked to dairy, although they do not come from cows.

- Always buy eggs fresh and do not hold more than a week's stock, as eggs deteriorate with age. Their shells are porous – eggs slowly dry out and lose flavour.
- Always tell the supplier what size eggs you want – they can be small, medium, large and very large.
- Never wash any dirt off an egg shell, as you will be washing dirt into the egg.
- Cracked eggs should not be used as they may be contaminated.
- Store eggs in a cool, dry place away from strong smells. If they are kept in a fridge always take them out at least an hour before use so they can develop their flavour.
- If using eggs in baking, eggs at room temperature will mix in more easily and give a better result than those straight from a fridge.

Eggs

Fruit and vegetables

Fruit

In catering we use the term fruit to mean the edible part of a plant that is served as a sweet dish or to accompany a sweet dish. These are often classified into hard and soft fruit. Hard fruits include apples, pears and similar. Soft fruits include plums, strawberries and similar.

As soft fruit goes off very quickly, only buy enough for a day or two at a time, otherwise it might go off and be unusable.

Fruit

Potatoes

One of the most versatile vegetables is the potato. It is a **tuber** and grows underground.

There are many varieties of potato, and some of the more popular are shown here along with how they are best cooked. In general those with a waxy texture are best for baking and those with a floury texture are best for chips.

As most caterers cannot carry a lot of different potatoes, two good all-round potatoes are Desiree and King Edward.

> **Key words**
>
> **Tuber** – a swollen, fleshy part of a plant's stem that usually grows underground.

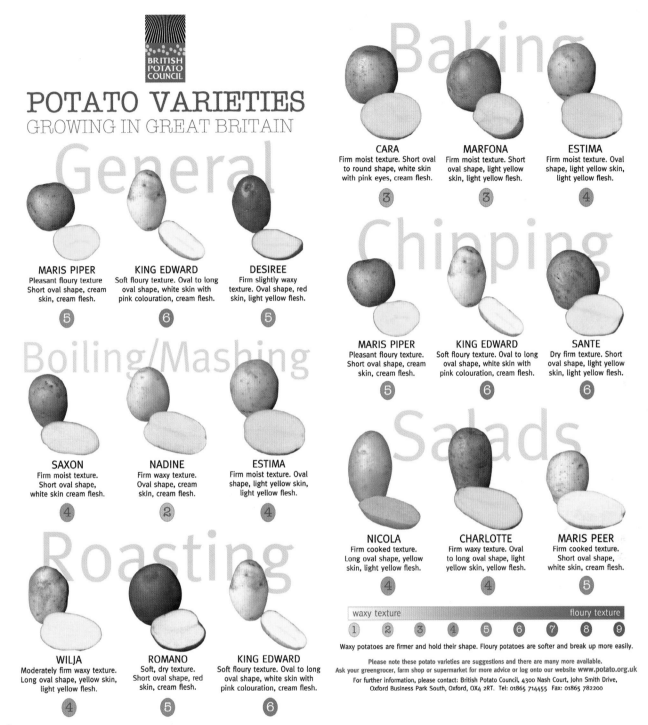

Types of potato

Vegetables

In catering we use the term vegetable to mean the edible part of a plant that is served as a savoury dish or to accompany a savoury dish. These may be

the roots, leaves, flowers or fruit of the plant. Mushrooms are included as a vegetable, although they are a fungus. Some of the more popular vegetables are listed in Table 6.6.

Table 6.6 Common vegetables and their main cooking methods

Name	Part of plant	Main cooking methods
Broad beans	Fruit	Boiling, steaming
Runner beans	Fruit	Boiling, steaming
Broccoli	Flower	Boiling, steaming, stir-fry
Cabbage	Leaves	Boiling, steaming, stir-fry
Carrots	Roots	Boiling, steaming, roasting
Cauliflower	Flower	Boiling, steaming, stir-fry
Courgettes	Fruit	Boiling, steaming, frying
Mushrooms	Fungus	Frying, grilling, boiling

	Part of plant	Main cooking methods
Onions	Bulb	Frying, braising
Parsnips	Roots	Boiling, steaming, roasting
Peas	Fruit	Boiling, steaming
Peppers	Fruit	Boiling, steaming, roasting, grilling
Tomatoes	Fruit	roasting, grilling

Buying fruit and vegetables

- Most caterers purchase fruit and vegetables from a wholesale greengrocer, who will carry a wide stock of items and will deliver daily. Wholesalers purchase their fruit and vegetables from a variety of sources, including direct from the grower and also from wholesale markets, which are found in many large cities. They may source some of their items locally and these can be mentioned on the menu.
- Smaller catering businesses may buy from a local greengrocer as they only need small quantities. By ordering in advance they will be able to purchase at a price lower than the normal retail price. The greengrocer will normally purchase their items from a market or a wholesaler.
- All fruit and vegetables should be ripe, fresh looking, firm, and without bruises or other marks. Check them carefully to ensure that they have no damage.

Storing fruit and vegetables

Most fruit and vegetables can be stored in a cool, dry room.

Leave potatoes in their sacks, as they keep best in darker conditions. If they are in the light they can develop a slight green tinge. Always remove this before cooking, as it is mildly poisonous.

Most salad items, green vegetables and soft fruit are best stored at about 8°C, which is just a bit warmer than a normal fridge. Always remove these items from the fridge if they are going to be eaten cold to allow them to warm up and the flavour to develop.

Never put bananas in the fridge – they will go black.

Keep strawberries and other soft fruits in the punnets they are delivered in, and keep other soft fruit in trays. Do not stack soft fruit on top of each other as this can bruise them.

Activity

1 What fresh vegetables are in season in the UK in November?
2 How should fresh root vegetables be stored?
3 Where should salad vegetables be stored?
4 What would you check for when receiving a delivery of fresh vegetables?
5 Find an interesting recipe that uses at least five vegetables.

Pasta, grains, beans and pulses

Pasta

Pasta is made from durum wheat, flour, eggs and oil, and is a traditional Italian food. Durum wheat is about 15 per cent protein and about 80 per cent carbohydrate. This is why it is popular with athletes such as rowers, who need both of these items in their diet.

Pasta is very similar to noodles, which are used in Asian cuisine, but these are normally made from rice flour.

Dried pasta has a very long shelf life and does not deteriorate with age. There are over 100 different pasta shapes, some of the more popular being spaghetti, macaroni, conchiglie, lasagne and penne.

Capelleti, ravioli and cannelloni are examples of filled pasta, and filings may include meat, ham, cheese and spinach.

Do not overcook pasta; it should be *al dente* (which means 'with a bit of bite' or firm) when cooked, not soft and mushy. If you are cooking pasta that will later be served cold, always rinse it under cold water to stop it cooking and let it drain.

Some pasta varieties

Rice

This is one of the most widely found foods and is eaten by half the world's population. It needs a moist, hot atmosphere to produce it, so it is mainly grown in India, Asia, South America, Italy and the USA.

There are hundreds of rice varieties; the most common ones used are:

- **Long grain** – this has had the outer bran removed; when cooked the grains tend to stay separate. It is served with savoury dishes such as curries, chilli con carne and stuffed peppers.
- **Short grain** – this rice used for dishes that require the grains to stick together, such a rice pudding and risotto.
- **Brown rice** – this rice has had its outer covering removed but still has the bran layers (which are brown). It has a nutty flavour when cooked.
- **Basmati rice** – this Indian long grain rice goes well with curries and similar dishes.

Rice

Cooked rice must be stored carefully if being kept to be served cold. Rice can contain **Bacillus cereus**, which is found in soil, and it is has **spores** that are not killed by the cooking process. If it is not kept in a fridge these spores can germinate and produce a **toxin** that can cause serious food poisoning: it can be fatal. Never keep cooked rice for more than 2 days in a fridge and, if put out on a buffet, it is best to throw away any uneaten rice.

Other grains

- **Sweetcorn/maize** is often served as corn on the cob, either as an accompaniment to a main course or as a starter. It is also made into popcorn and cornflakes.
- **Oats**, often served as porridge for breakfast, can also be used to coat fish before shallow frying. It can be baked into oatcakes and added to bread to give it a different texture and flavour.
- **Wheat** is the basis of most flours used in cookery. It can either be plain or processed to make it self-raising flour. Strong wheat flour, such a durum, is used in bread making. Wheat can also be used to make semolina and couscous.

Dried beans and pulses

The term **pulse** refers to any crops that are harvested solely for the dried grain. This does not include green beans and peas, which are classified as vegetables.

In general pulses are about 20–25 per cent protein, as well as having carbohydrate and fibre. They are also low in fat. Many vegetarians eat a lot of pulses to help them eat a balanced diet.

Beans and pulses

Because pulses are dried, most of them need soaking before cooking, which can take anything from 4 to 12 hours. This is usually done overnight in a fridge with plenty of water. They will absorb some of the water and gradually expand.

Dried red kidney beans are toxic and can kill unless treated correctly:

1   Soak in water for at least 8 hours.
2   Drain and cook in fresh boiling water for at least 10 minutes.
3   Simmer for another hour.

Buying pasta, grains, beans and pulses

■   Most caterers will buy pasta, grains, dried beans and pulses from a wholesale grocer. They normally carry a large range of items in different sized packs to suit different catering firms.
■   Most pulses are bought as dried beans and stored in airtight containers. Some pulses can be purchased in tins and simply drained before use and added to dishes straight away. Red kidney beans, borlotti beans and broad beans are all available in tins.

Storing pasta, grains, beans and pulses

These are all dried items and should be kept in sealed containers in the stores. They all have a long shelf life, but do check the dates before use. Tinned items will have a best-before date on the tin.

If using fresh pasta, store it in a fridge.

Activity

1   Visit your local supermarket and see how many pulses they have for sale.
2   Either find an interesting recipe that uses one of these pulses *or* find a recipe that uses black-eyed beans.
3   Which rice would you use for a rice pudding, and why?
4   What is the correct method of cooking red kidney beans?
5   What are the main nutrients found in pasta?

Convenience foods

This term is used to describe any foods that have undergone some process to make them either easier or quicker to use. This can save on labour costs for the caterer and reduce the amount of basic preparation done, leaving more time for chefs to use their cooking skills.

The disadvantage is that the price of these items can be quite high, especially as there is extra packaging to pay for, and they are not often good value for money.

Some of the more common ones used in the catering industry include:

- frozen vegetables and chips
- fresh or frozen prepared meat dishes, such as kebabs and chicken kievs; some of these will have been made from the cheaper cuts of meat
- tinned food including meat, fruit and vegetables
- pre-packed salads and stir frys
- instant coffee, stock cubes, gravy powder and instant custard, which all just need hot or boiling water to be added to them
- cake mixes
- easy-cook rice
- dried vegetables.

Health issues

Because many of these foods have been designed for a long shelf life, they may contain large amounts of preservatives, saturated fats, sugar and salt. When using convenience foods always check the labels to see what has been added.

If people rely on a lot of convenience food in their diet, it is likely they will reduce the amount of fresh fruit and vegetables they eat, which can reduce the amount of vitamin C they eat and lead to health problems.

Convenience foods

Professional tip

Always check the contents of convenience food before use, and adjust your recipe accordingly. You may need to experiment to obtain the best results.

Activity

1 Buy a tin of split pea soup and compare the ingredients with Recipe 4 in Chapter 4.
2 Make fresh split pea soup and compare the taste and texture with the tinned soup.
3 Work out how much it costs to make the fresh split pea soup and compare this with the price of the tinned soup.
4 Which would you serve in a restaurant?

Local suppliers

Some smaller caterers might use local suppliers for their fresh ingredients rather than the main wholesalers. This might include local butchers, greengrocers, delicatessens and farm shops.

Advertising where you buy from lets customers know that your food is fresh and local. The customers will see that they are supporting local trade, and keeping the money in the area, not buying from a business many miles away. It will also give some publicity to these local suppliers, and the customers may also use them for their own purchases. The restaurant could also advertise at their local suppliers to bring in new local customers. In this way the supplier and the business can support each other.

Using local suppliers can also help with deliveries, with any extra items that are needed being obtained quickly. It will also reduce the **food miles** and possibly the **carbon footprint** of the food.

Activity

Why would an independent restaurant use a local butcher rather than a wholesale one?

Stretch yourself

1 Make a comparison of fresh and ready-made pastry:
   (a) Buy a packet of ready-made sweet pastry and make an apple pie.
   (b) Make some fresh sweet pastry and make an apple pie.
   (c) Hold a blind tasting in the college canteen and see which people prefer and why.
2 Imagine that you are going to open a restaurant near to where you live. You need to find some suppliers and have decided to use local ones where possible.
   (a) Investigate what local suppliers you could use for meat, fish, fruit and vegetables, and bread.
   (b) If possible, visit one of the suppliers and see what their range of products is.

Chapter 7

Using kitchen equipment

Learning objectives

By the end of this chapter you will:
- Know about different types of kitchen equipment
- Be able to select and use kitchen equipment, including knives
- Be able to clean knives, equipment and work surfaces safely and hygienically

In this chapter you will learn about some of the more common types of equipment, large and small, used in the hospitality and catering industry.

This chapter takes you through the stages of food production, from storage through to cleaning after service, looking at the equipment used at each stage.

Health and safety

- Never use any equipment you have not been trained to use.
- Always ensure that you are wearing the correct personal protective equipment (PPE), such as chef's whites with long sleeves and safety shoes, before using equipment.
- Remember to use a clean, dry oven cloth when handling hot pots, pans and baking trays. Keep one handy when you are cooking.

Large equipment

Refrigerators and chill rooms

Refrigerators and chill rooms keep food chilled at between 1 °C and 5 °C. These cold conditions slow down the growth of bacteria that make food go 'off'. They are used to store a whole range of products.

Cleaning refrigerators and chill rooms: chill rooms and refrigerators must be tidied once a day and cleaned out once

a week. Clean with hot water and suitable cleaning chemicals – diluted bicarbonate of soda is most suitable.

Freezers

Freezers are used to store food at between –18°C and –20°C. Food in the freezer does not last indefinitely, but the low temperature slows down the growth of bacteria and means that the food will last longer.

Cleaning freezers: most modern freezers are frost-free, which means that they do not need to be defrosted. Tidy the freezer at least once a week. Clean it out every three to six months using a mild cleaning fluid, mild detergent or diluted bicarbonate of soda.

Tables

These should be stainless steel, with a shelf at the bottom to store items on and a drawer to keep small equipment in safely. Many will have a small up-stand at the back to stop food going down the back. They should be on lockable wheels, so they can be pulled out and the walls and floor around them cleaned properly.

Cleaning tables: always clean as you go while preparing food; use the correct cleaner, such as D10 or similar, to ensure that surfaces are sanitised.

Sinks

A kitchen must have at least one sink for staff to wash their hands in before and during work. This must have hot water, soap, a towel or hand drier, and a nail brush. The best ones have a knee-operated tap so that you do not have to touch the tap with dirty hands. Dirty taps can spread bacteria.

Washing-up sinks should be stainless steel with a sloping draining board to help items dry. The detergent should be in an automatic dispenser, which is the most economic and effective way to ensure that the correct amount of detergent is used.

Solid top stoves

These are also known as solid top hobs and are made of solid metal with a burner. They have a single flat surface, meaning saucepans can be moved around easily during cooking. The middle of the hob has intense heat; the side is not so hot and is used to simmer.

Solid top hobs may be gas or electric. Gas-operated hobs have removable rings in the centre, which can be removed to expose the flame and allow the chef to place the saucepan directly on to the flame. This intense heat allows the food to cook faster or liquid to reduce quickly.

Cleaning solid top hobs: remove all food debris, clean with hot detergent water, dry and lightly oil.

Range stoves

Gas

These are gas stoves where the flame is exposed; the saucepans are placed on metal bars over the flame. It is more difficult to move the saucepans

around on this type of hob than on solid top hobs. To simmer, the flame has to be reduced using a switch that controls each flame.

Cleaning open range hobs: remove the metal bars, wash in hot detergent water and dry. Clean the stove surface with hot detergent water after removing any food debris; a light abrasive may be required for any baked-on food. Dry and replace metal bars.

Electric

These will have separate hobs, each with a switch to control the heat. Many of these cookers have a ceramic top but some may still have separate metal rings or solid plates.

Cleaning electric hobs: it is safest to switch the cooker off at the mains before cleaning to avoid any danger of an electric shock. Clean ceramic hobs with hot detergent water and a cloth; remove any burnt-on food with a metal scraper.

Induction hobs

The burners on induction hobs are called induction coils. The coil only heats up when a pan with a metal base (such as a stainless steel pan) is in direct contact with the hob. When the pan is removed from the hob it turns off straight away and cools down quickly. The hob will still feel slightly warm after it is turned off.

Water boils rapidly on an induction hob and overall food cooks more quickly than on other types of hobs. They are also very efficient in their use of power, and a kitchen with induction hobs will stay cooler than one with traditional stoves.

Cleaning induction hobs: induction hobs are very easy to clean and usually require only a wipe down with mild detergent water.

Ovens

Conventional ovens

A large variety of conventional ovens are available, which are fuelled by either gas or electricity. Some have grills built in.

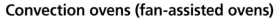

Health and safety

With gas ovens, it is very important to light the gas once it is turned on. Gas ovens and ranges must be fitted with a flame-failure device. This switches off the gas if the flame blows out, to prevent an explosion.

Convection ovens (fan-assisted ovens)

These ovens have a built-in fan, which circulates hot air around the oven. This evens out the temperature in all parts of the oven, making it more efficient and meaning that cooking temperatures can be lowered. For example, something that would have to be cooked at 200°C in a conventional oven might cook at 180°C in a convection oven. Convection ovens are very good for baking and roasting.

Cleaning conventional and convection ovens: allow the equipment to cool before scrubbing it down and wiping it clean. Apply a little oil to the surface of solid tops.

Health and safety

When cleaning, always use protective clothing and allow the equipment to cool down first to avoid accidental burns. Always wear a safety mask when using a chemical oven cleaner.

Combination ovens

Combination ovens can be used as an oven, a steamer or both. Steam is injected into the oven when you are baking and roasting to increase the moisture content (humidity) of the oven. Combination ovens can be fuelled by gas or electricity. They are fully automatic, having built-in computers that can be pre-programmed to cook food for exactly the right amount of time, and they are also able to keep food at the correct temperature. The latest versions monitor the internal temperature of the food, allowing the chef to achieve exact core temperature and deliver precise cooking textures. A computer system also records how often the oven is used and the temperatures used.

Cleaning combination ovens: many modern models are self-cleaning, but they need to be checked regularly to make sure the cleaning programme is efficient.

Health and safety

Take care when removing trays from the oven. When using a combination oven as a steamer, make sure that you release the steam gently before opening the door.

Microwave ovens

Microwave ovens use high-frequency power. The energy waves disturb the molecules in food and move them, causing friction and heating the food. Microwave ovens can cook food more quickly than conventional ovens. They are often used for reheating food.

Cleaning microwave ovens: clean up spillages immediately with hot, mild detergent water. This prevents bacteria growing and reduces the risk of contaminating other foods.

Health and safety

Microwave ovens should be inspected regularly. If the door seal is damaged, do not use the microwave and report it to your employer or manager immediately.

Metal should never be used in a microwave unless it has a metal reflector. Using metal in a microwave without a metal reflector causes sparks and small explosions in the oven.

Steamers

- **Atmospheric steamer** – operates at normal atmospheric pressure (the same pressure as outside the steamer), creating steam at just above 100°C. These are often normal saucepans with a metal basket in them.
- **Pressure steamers** – a good way to cook delicate food and foods cooked in a pouch. Some pressure steamers cook at high pressure and some at low pressure. In low-pressure steamers, the temperature of the steam is 70°C and so food is cooked slowly. In high-pressure steamers, the temperature of the steam is 120°C and so food is cooked faster.

- **Dual steamers** – these can switch between low and high pressure. At low pressure they cook in the same way as pressure steamers. At high pressure the food is cooked more quickly than atmospheric steamers and pressure steamers.

All steamers are available in a variety of sizes.

Combination ovens can also be used to combine steaming and conventional oven cooking to get the benefits of both.

Cleaning steamers: steamers have to be cleaned regularly. The inside of the steamer, trays and runners should be washed in hot detergent water, then rinsed and dried. Door controls should be lightly greased occasionally and the door left slightly open to allow air to circulate when the steamer is not in use. If water is held in the steamer then it must be changed regularly. The water chamber should be drained and cleaned before fresh water is added.

In hard water areas a steamer may need to be descaled, to remove the build-up of calcium. This is just like descaling your kettle at home. If it is not removed, the heating element becomes less efficient and is more likely to need replacing.

Health and safety

The main safety hazard associated with steamers is scalding. Take care when opening steamer doors: open the door slowly to allow the steam to escape gradually from the oven, then carefully remove the food items.

Before use, check that the steamer is clean and safe to use. Any faults must be reported immediately.

Deep-fat fryers

A deep-fat fryer has a container with enough oil in it to cover the food. The oil is heated to very hot temperatures. A cool zone, which is a chamber at the base of the cooking pan, collects odd bits of food such as breadcrumbs or batter from fish when it is being fried.

Some fryers are computerised; these can be programmed to heat the oil to the correct temperature and cook the food for the right amount of time.

Cleaning a deep-fat fryer: when frying, remove all the food debris immediately and keep the oil as clean as possible. You will need to remove the oil to clean the fryer. Make sure the oil is cool before removing it and put suitable containers in place to drain the oil into. Replace with clean oil.

Griddle

A griddle is a solid cooking surface that is heated from below. The food is cooked directly on the griddle surface. Some griddles have a corrugated surface, which is good for cooking steaks, fish and burgers, while others have a flat surface for cooking eggs; some will have both. A griddle will usually slope down from the back to the front so that fat can drain away into a tray or container.

A smaller griddle plate can also be put on to a cooking range, and this is how Welsh cakes and tortillas are traditionally made.

Cleaning griddles: griddles have a tray to catch grease and food debris. This needs to be emptied and thoroughly cleaned with hot detergent water. Soda is very useful for removing grease. The surface needs to be cleaned according to the manufacturer's guidelines, but most should be wiped with clean oil once they are clean.

Grills

Salamander

A salamander (also known as an overhead grill) is heated from above by gas or electricity. Most salamanders have more than one set of heating elements or jets, and it is not always necessary to have them all fully turned on.

Cleaning salamanders: salamanders have a tray to catch grease and food debris. This needs to be emptied and thoroughly cleaned with hot detergent water. Soda is very useful for removing grease.

Under-fired (under-heated) grills

The heat source for these is underneath the grill. Under-fired grills are used to cook food quickly, so they need to reach a high temperature. This type of grill makes criss-cross marks on the food, known as **quadrillage**.

Cleaning under-fired grills: when the bars are cool, they should be removed and washed in hot water containing a grease solvent (detergent). They should then be rinsed, dried and replaced in the grill. If firebricks are used for lining the grill, take care with these as they break easily.

Quadrillage

Contact grills

These are sometimes called double-sided grills or infragrills. They have two heating surfaces that face each other. The food is placed on one surface and is then covered by the second. These grills are electrically heated and cook certain foods, such a toast in a toaster, very quickly.

Cleaning contact grills: turn off the electricity when cleaning and avoid using water. Lightly scrape clean.

Hot cupboards

Commonly referred to as a hotplate, a hot cupboard is used for heating plates and serving dishes, and for keeping food hot. You must make sure that the temperature in the hot cupboard is kept at around 63–70 °C so that the food is not too hot or too cold. Hot cupboards may be heated by gas, steam or electricity.

Cleaning hot cupboards: hot cupboards must be emptied and cleaned after each service.

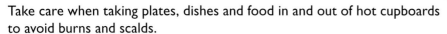

Health and safety

Take care when taking plates, dishes and food in and out of hot cupboards to avoid burns and scalds.

Bain-marie

Traditionally these are open wells of water for keeping food hot, but there are also dry heat bain-maries. The food is put into containers which are then placed above the heat source, or into the hot water. Bain-maries are available in many designs, some of which are built into hot cupboards and some into serving controls. They are heated by steam, gas or electricity.

Cleaning bain-maries: turn the heat off after use. Drain the water away and clean the bain-marie inside and out with hot detergent water. Then rinse it and dry it. If it has a drain-off tap, this should be closed.

Health and safety

It is important never to allow a water-based bain-marie to run dry when the heat is turned on.

Be careful when putting containers in a water-based bain-marie as the water will be hot and can scald you. Check the temperature regularly: never allow it to differ from the recipe and safety requirements.

Dishwasher

Most catering businesses use heavy-duty dishwashers to clean cutlery, crockery, pots and pans. They wash at between 65 °C and 71 °C, which is hotter than washing by hand. The dishes are sanitised either through an 82 °C final rinse or through the use of a chemical sanitiser.

Commercial dishwashers do not have a drying cycle. When the washed items are taken out of the dishwasher they air dry very quickly because they are so hot. This is quicker and more hygienic than drying with cloths.

Cleaning dishwashers: all dishwashers will have a tray or filter to catch food debris, which must be emptied and cleaned after use. Wipe the outside of the dishwasher with a mild detergent. Ensure the dishwasher is drained and leave the cover open to help it dry out.

Health and safety

Dishwashers use very powerful detergents, so be careful not to get any on your hands. Never use dishwasher detergent for hand-washing pots and pans; it will damage your skin and could cause a rash.

Food waste disposer

All catering businesses have to deal with waste food, especially from customers' plates. One way of dealing with it is to have a waste disposal unit plumbed into the wash-up area. All food scraps are put into this unit, which then grinds or chops the food up until it is small enough to be washed away into the drains. It is then dealt with at the sewage works and, in some cases, can be used to produce fertiliser and methane gas, both of which are then sold to make money.

Cleaning a waste disposal unit: the outside should be kept clean with mild detergent, but the inside is self-cleaning in operation.

Health and safety

Make sure the cover is used, if the machine has one, and never put your hand in to unblock it. Always call maintenance to do this.

Do not put anything but food into the unit. Be very careful with teaspoons, which can be dropped in accidentally.

Knives and cutting equipment

Knives

The professional chef will use a whole range of knives in the kitchen; each type of knife is used for a specific job and skill. It is important that knives are used safely and efficiently.

Boning knives are short-bladed knives used for boning meat. The blade is strong and rigid, with a pointed end. The inflexible blade allows the chef to get close to the bones and cut away the meat.

Butcher's saws are commonly used in butchery to saw through bones.

Carving knives and forks – a French carving knife has a long, thin blade and is known as a tranchard. A carving fork is two-pronged. It is strong enough to support meats for carving, and to lift them to and from containers.

Chopping knives are used for a variety of jobs, such as chopping, cutting, slicing and shredding vegetables, meat and fruit.

Filleting knives are used for filleting fish (removing the meat from the bones). They have a very flexible blade, which allows the chef to move the knife easily around the bone structure of fish.

Meat cleavers are also known as choppers and are usually used for chopping bones.

Paring knives (also known as **office knives**) are small, multipurpose vegetable knives. They are used for topping and tailing vegetables, and for peeling certain fruit and vegetables.

Palette knives are flat for lifting and scraping, turning and spreading. They are also useful when making pastry products.

Serrated-edge carving knives are used for slicing foods. They have a long, thick serrated blade, which is used in a sawing action. These knives are not sharpened in the kitchen – they have to be sent to a specialist company to be sharpened.

Turning knives have a small curved blade. They are used for shaping vegetables in a variety of ways.

Other cutting equipment

A **carborundum** is used for sharpening knives.

Corers are used to remove the fibrous core from fruit such as apples, pineapples and pears. They have a rounded blade, which you push down into the centre of the fruit to cut through the fruit around the core. The core stays tightly inside the corer and is removed from the fruit when you pull it out.

Food processors are electrical machines used for many jobs in the kitchen. They usually come with a range of blades for cutting, puréeing and mixing.

Graters are made from stainless steel. They come in various sizes and are used to shred and grate food such as cheese, the zest of citrus fruits and vegetables. Graters usually have a choice of grating edges: fine, medium or large.

Gravity-feed slicers have very sharp cutting blades and must be operated with a safety guard. They are used for slicing meat so that every slice is the same thickness.

Kitchen scissors are used for a number of purposes in the kitchen. Fish scissors are used for cutting fins from fish. Poultry scissors are used to portion poultry.

Mandolins are specialist pieces of equipment used for slicing vegetables. The blade is made from stainless steel and is adjustable to different widths, for thick or thin slices of food. They are usually used to slice vegetables such as potatoes, courgettes, cucumbers and carrots. The blade is particularly sharp, so you should be very careful when using one. Modern mandolins have an in-built safety guard.

Mincers can be stand-alone or attachments that fit on to a mixer. They have a circular cutting blade that forces the food through a plate with different sized holes depending on the size of mince required.

Peelers are used for peeling certain vegetables and fruit.

Steels are used for sharpening knives. They are cylindrical pieces of steel with a handle at one end. To sharpen a knife, run the blade at an angle along the steel edge.

Whetstones are also used for sharpening knives.

Safe use of knives

Knives are essential tools for all chefs, but they can cause serious injury to the user or to someone else if used incorrectly or carelessly. Knives that are looked after and treated with care will give good service and will be less likely to cause injury.

By following a few simple rules you should be able to avoid serious injury from knives and keep accidental cuts to an absolute minimum. Use your knives correctly at all times.

- Hold a cook's knife with your finger around the handle (thumb and index fingers on opposite sides) and well clear of the blade edge. This will sometimes vary depending on the size and design of the knife you are using and the task you are carrying out.
- Grasp the knife firmly for full control.
- Always make sure that the fingers and thumb of the hand not holding the knife are well tucked in to avoid cutting them.
- If carrying a knife in the kitchen, hold it to the side of your body with the blade pointing downwards and backwards.
- Never run while holding a knife.
- When handing a knife to someone else, offer them the handle while you hold the top (blunt edge) of the blade.
- Keep the blade away from you when cleaning or drying knives, and never run your finger along the blade edge.
- Do not have more than one knife at a time on a chopping board. When not using a knife, place it at the side of the board with the blade pointing in. Never carry knives around on top of chopping boards because they could slide off.
- Do not let knives overhang the edge of the work surface; they could be knocked off or fall and cause injury. Never try to catch a falling knife; stand back until it reaches the floor.
- Never leave a knife on a surface with the blade pointing outwards. You or someone else could put their hand down on the blade of the knife.
- Never place knives in washing-up water; the blade will not be visible so someone could put their hands in the water and cut themselves.
- Keep the handle of the knife clean and dry. If the handle is greasy or wet it could slip in your hands during use.
- Keep knives visible, i.e. not under vegetable peelings or a dishcloth.

Maintenance and care of knives

Sharpening

Knives that are kept sharp are safer than blunt knives, provided that they are handled with care. This is because a sharp knife will cut efficiently and cleanly without needing too much pressure to cut through the food. A blunt knife is less easy to control; it will need more pressure and force, and is likely to slip sideways, possibly causing injury as well as poorly prepared food.

Keep knives sharp by sharpening them frequently with a steel or other sharpening tool. Make sure that you are shown how to do this safely.

If a knife has become very blunt it may need to be reground by someone who specialises in doing this. An electric or manually operated grinding wheel can be used to replace the lost 'edge' on the knife. Arrangements can be made for mobile units to visit your premises to regrind knives, or they can be sent away to be reground.

Some chefs use a sharpening stone.

Cleaning

A knife can very easily transfer harmful bacteria from one place to another, becoming a 'vehicle' of contamination. Follow a few simple rules to avoid this:

- Wash and dry knives thoroughly between tasks.
- Do not use the same cloth to clean knives between tasks, especially when you are preparing raw or high-risk foods.
- If you have used a knife on raw meat or poultry, be sure to disinfect it before using it for another task. Detergents remove the grease, but disinfectants kill harmful bacteria.
- When you have finished working with a knife, wash it thoroughly with hot detergent water, then rinse it, dry it and put it away. Bacteria will multiply on dirty or wet knives.

Professional tip

Take great care of your knives; always keep them clean. There are a variety of knives on the market – some have handles made of easy-to-clean material.

Storage

Store knives carefully, preferably in a box or carrying case with compartments to keep the knives separate and make them easy to find. Do not just throw knives loosely into a drawer or locker.

Age restrictions specific to the use of cutting equipment

There are age restrictions for the use of potentially dangerous equipment in the kitchen, such as gravity-feed slicing machines; you must be over 18 to use them.

Activity

1. It is important to use knives and cutting equipment correctly to prevent accidents and injury to yourself and others. Give four other reasons why it is important to use knives and cutting equipment correctly.
2. Identify the following knives and state what they are used for:

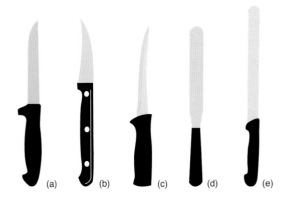

(a)　(b)　(c)　(d)　(e)

3. Why should you not use blunt knives?
4. How can a professional knife be sharpened?
5. What is the legal age for a person to use a gravity-feed slicing machine?
6. What would you use a mandolin for?

Small equipment and utensils

Each piece of small equipment has a specific use in the kitchen. Small equipment and utensils are made from a variety of materials, including non-stick coated metal, iron, steel and heatproof plastic. Small equipment must be looked after, cleaned and stored safely and hygienically.

Bowls come in various sizes and can be stainless steel or plastic. They are used for a variety of purposes including mixing, blending and storing food.

Colanders are available in a variety of sizes and usually made from stainless steel. They are used for draining liquids.

Conical strainers are usually stainless steel with large mesh. They are used for general straining and passing of liquids, soups and sauces.

Cooling racks are made from stainless steel mesh and are usually rectangular. Baked items are placed on cooling racks to cool. The mesh allows air to circulate, enabling the items to cool quickly.

Cutlet bats are made from metal and used to bat out meat.

Flan rings are used to make flan cases and flans. The flan ring is lined with pastry to make the pastry case, then filled with the flan mixture or tart filling.

Fish slices are made from stainless steel. They are used for lifting and sliding food on and off trays to serving dishes.

Food mixers are labour-saving electrical devices used for many different tasks in the kitchen. They have a range of attachments for different jobs such as mincing, cutting, blending and mixing.

Ladles come in various sizes. They are large, scoop-shaped spoons used to add liquids to cooking pots, and to serve sauces and stews.

Liquidisers and blenders are pieces of mechanical equipment used to blend solid food into liquids. They can be made from glass, plastic or stainless steel.

Mashers can be manual or electric and are used for mashing vegetables.

Measuring jugs are available in a variety of sizes. They can be made from stainless steel, glass or plastic. They are used for measuring liquids.

Moulds come in many shapes and sizes. They are used for shaping and moulding food for presentation, for example tartlets, mousses, custards and blancmange. Moulds are very difficult to clean – you must make sure that all food debris is removed and that the mould is cleaned properly to prevent cross-contamination.

Rolling pins are used for rolling pastry manually. Today they are usually made from plastic.

Scales are used to weigh ingredients.

Sieves are made from plastic with a nylon mesh. They are available in various sizes. They are a type of strainer and can be used to sieve dry ingredients, such as flour, or for purées.

Skimming spoons are made from stainless steel and have holes in them. They are used for skimming and draining. Skimming is removing fat and other unwanted substances from the top of liquids, such as stocks and soups.

Spiders are made from stainless steel. They are used for removing food from containers, saucepans, water, and so on. They are also used to remove food from a deep-fat fryer.

Spoons come in variety of sizes for serving and moving food to and from containers. They are made from stainless steel.

Whisks are wired and used for whisking and beating air into products, for example, whisking egg whites. Heavier wired whisks are available for whisking sauces.

Care, cleanliness and storage

Thoroughly wash all equipment, pans and utensils with detergent and hot water after use. Rinse with hot water and then dry thoroughly. Incomplete cleaning and drying can lead to build-up of mould, food contamination and cross-contamination.

Health and safety

Always make sure that the safety guards are in place before using mechanical equipment. Report any faulty equipment to your line manager or supervisor. Always make sure that mechanical equipment is serviced regularly and maintained in good working order.

Cutting boards

These are used for chopping and slicing food on. The most popular boards are made from polyethylene or plastic. Different boards should be used for different foods to avoid cross-contamination. The accepted UK system is:

Cutting boards must be stored correctly in a safe and hygienic way, preferably on a rack allowing the circulation of air so that, after they have been thoroughly cleaned, they are allowed to dry and other types of boards or equipment cannot contaminate them. Incorrect storage of boards may lead to cross-contamination and food poisoning.

Cooking pans

Baking sheets are made in various sizes from black wrought steel. They are used for baking and pastry work.

Baking tins (sometimes called cake tins) are used for baking cakes, bread and sponges. The mixture is placed in the tin before cooking.

Griddle pans have raised ribs to mark the food. The griddle lines (quadrillage) give the food a chargrilled effect. Modern griddle pans have a non-stick surface.

Non-stick frying pans are coated with a material such as Teflon, which prevents the food from sticking to them. They are usually used for shallow frying.

Roasting trays are metal trays, usually made of stainless steel. They have deep sides and are used for roasting food such as meat and vegetables.

Saucepans come in various sizes and are made in a variety of materials. Some are made solely of stainless steel; others contain a mixture of metals such as stainless steel with an aluminium layer and a thick copper coil. Saucepans are used for a variety of cooking methods, including boiling, poaching and stewing.

Sauté pans are shallow, straight-sided pans made from stainless steel or a mixture of metals. They are used for shallow frying when a sauce is made after the food is fried. They may also be used for poaching, especially for shallow-poached fish.

Woks are shallow, rounded frying pans used for stir-frying and oriental cookery. They are made from material that can conduct heat quickly. Thick copper-core stainless steel is the most effective.

Health and safety

Incorrect pan storage can result in pans falling from the shelves, causing injury and damage to the equipment. Store pans upside down on clean racks. Check that handles are not loose.

Items stored at a great height may cause people to stretch, causing back strain. Minimise the risk by storing pans at a lower level, so that people do not need to stretch for them.

Activity

1 What colour board should you use to prepare wet fish?
2 Give two reasons why it is important not to use a saucepan that is too large for the food being cooked.

Chapter 8 — Safety, hygiene and security

Learning objectives

By the end of this chapter you will:
- Know how to maintain personal health and hygiene
- Know how to maintain a hygienic, safe and secure workplace

It is important to follow the correct procedures to ensure that your work environment is safe, hygienic and secure. Everyone at work has a role to play in this and, by working together, accidents can be prevented, people will be safe and the business will be more productive.

Personal uniform and dress standards, as well as personal hygiene, are covered in detail in Chapter 10. This chapter focuses on the Health and Safety at Work Act and how to deal with accidents and emergencies.

The Health and Safety at Work Act 1974

Under this legislation both employers and employees have responsibilities to ensure that workplaces are safe. The hospitality industry is one of most dangerous workplaces in the country, with heat, slippery surfaces and sharp knives, so this is a very important piece of legislation.

Employer responsibilities

Employers have a responsibility to provide a safe workplace that will not cause employees illness or harm. This means:
- premises themselves are safe, with good lighting and ventilation

- equipment must be tested for safety and maintained correctly
- chemicals must be stored and used correctly and staff trained in how to do this
- **risk assessments** must have been completed
- employees should receive a health and safety policy statement that outlines the employer's commitment to health and safety, and the measures in place to keep the workplace safe and comply with the law
- safety equipment and clothing must be provided
- staff should receive ongoing health and safety training.

If any of this is has not been explained to you where you work, then you need to ask about it.

Employee responsibilities

Employees have responsibilities too, and these are linked to the employer's responsibilities. As an employee you must:

- work in a safe way so that you do not endanger yourself or others working with you
- cooperate with the health and safety measures your employer has put in place
- wear the safety clothing and equipment provided
- report anything you notice that poses a health and safety risk or is potentially dangerous.

If you do something that endangers or hurts someone at work, an employer can discipline you or dismiss you, *and* you can be prosecuted for it, which can lead to a fine or even imprisonment.

Activity

1. What might happen to you if you ignore the health and safety rules put in place by your employer?
2. Name three of the responsibilities that an employee has for health and safety at work.
3. What are four responsibilities of employers under health and safety requirements?
4. Describe three health and safety-related matters you should report to a supervisor or line manager.
5. What is a health and safety policy statement? Why is it important to you at work?

What hazards might you find at work?

A **hazard** is something with the potential to cause harm. There are many different hazards in the hospitality and catering industry.

Equipment

- **Knives** – these are sharp and can cause serious injury. Keep your knives sharp, as a blunt knife is more likely to slip and cause injury in use. Always carry knives at your side with the point facing down and the sharp edge facing backwards.
- **Cookers** – these are hot, and you need to be particularly careful of gas flames on stoves and other equipment. If you find a stove is not working properly, tell your supervisor and other staff. Do not try to mend it yourself.

- **Pots and pans** – never put a pan handle over another ring or gas flame, and always point the handle away from the front of the cooker. This is to stop anyone knocking it when walking past. Always use a cloth when you take a pan off the stove. If the handle is still too hot to touch, warn any colleagues working close by and then either leave a cloth on the handle, or put some flour on the handle as a warning.
- **Steamers** – always release the pressure before opening the door as steam can cause very bad burns. Try to stand behind the door when you open the steamer, which will give you some protection.
- **Mixers and blenders** – never use these unless you have been trained. Large mixers can break your arm if it gets caught in it. Always use the guards supplied; if the guard is broken, tell your supervisor and do not use the machine. Stick blenders have sharp blades, which can cut off a finger, so use these carefully.
- Check the flex on portable equipment; if it shows any sign of damage it must be repaired or replaced.

Health and safety

If you are aware of anything in your workplace that could be a health and safety problem either put it right yourself (such as a wet floor) or report it to a supervisor (such as a faulty cable on a mixer).

Activity

1 Kitchen equipment can be dangerous and could cause harm if not used properly. List five items or areas that could be dangerous, the harm that could be caused and how it could be avoided.
2 If you need to use a mixing machine for the first time, what do you need to consider?

Hazardous substances

Cleaning chemicals – detergents, disinfectants, sanitisers, degreasers and descalers – are hazardous substances found in the workplace. Some of these are very powerful at removing grease from cookers and will also remove the oils from your skin. These can harm you through your skin, by getting in your eyes or if you breath them in.

■ Never use these chemicals unless you have been trained in how to use them and you are aware of the dangers.
■ Always read the instructions before use.
■ Wear **personal protective equipment (PPE)**, such as long-sleeved clothing, gloves or a face mask.
■ Treat the chemicals with care.

You might also come across fuel gels used for chafing dishes, and cooking liquids and gases, especially for outside events such as a barbeque.

The **Control of Substances Hazardous to Health (COSHH) Regulations** state that any substances or chemicals that could be hazardous to health must be:

■ stored, handled and disposed of according to COSHH regulations
■ identified on the packaging or container
■ identified in writing and given a risk rating so that safety precautions can be put in place
■ labelled appropriately as **toxic**, harmful, **irritant**, **corrosive**, explosive and/or oxidising.

Key words

Hazard – something with the potential to cause harm.

Risk – the likelihood of someone being harmed by the hazard.

Risk assessment – an examination of anything in the workplace that could harm people.

PPE – personal protective equipment; clothing and equipment that offers protection against hazards.

COSHH Regulations – Control of Substances Hazardous to Health regulations, which outline how any substances or chemicals that could be hazardous to health must be handled.

Corrosive

Flammable

Harmful

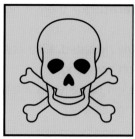
Toxic

Labels for hazardous chemicals

When using chemicals:

- make sure they are stored in a lockable cupboard away from the kitchen and not in direct sunlight
- store them in their original container, with the label in place and the top or lid firmly in place
- read instructions carefully and dilute exactly as directed
- never mix different chemicals
- if splashed on to skin, rinse with cold water and know the first aid procedures
- dispose of them in the required way.

Never play around with chemicals or spray them at anyone.

Activity

1 What do the letters COSHH stand for?
2 What is COSHH designed to do?

Work areas

- **Lighting** – this must be good enough to see to work safely, and any broken lights fixed. Accidents are more likely to happen in poorly lit areas.
- **Floors** – one of the main types of accidents in kitchens are trips and slips caused by wet or greasy floors. The person could fall on to something very hot, such as a deep-fat fryer or solid top stove, could spill something they are carrying on to themselves, such as a pan of hot soup, or could fall on to a sharp object such as a knife. They could also hit their head on a table or piece of equipment as they fall, or could fall on to moving machinery. Always clear up any spills; warn others of the spill and use warning signs as well.

- **Temperature** – there is no legal maximum working temperature, but you must have a supply of drinking water so that you can keep yourself properly hydrated. Kitchens can be very hot and you will lose water through sweating.
- **Noise** – if noise levels are too high you might not hear instructions or warnings clearly.

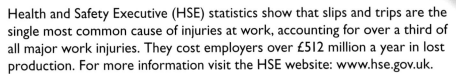

Health and safety

Health and Safety Executive (HSE) statistics show that slips and trips are the single most common cause of injuries at work, accounting for over a third of all major work injuries. They cost employers over £512 million a year in lost production. For more information visit the HSE website: www.hse.gov.uk.

Activity

1 What are three advantages of employers having good health and safety standards?
2 What is the most common cause of accidents in the hospitality industry? Suggest three ways these could be avoided.
3 Suggest four effects there could be on staff working in a kitchen with poor lighting and ventilation.
4 If someone slips, trips or falls in a kitchen, what are four injuries that could occur?

Stretch yourself

Identify any hazards at your work and see if you can eliminate them, perhaps by changing the layout of the kitchen or the workflow.

Personal clothing

- **Loose laces** – always tie up laces on boots and shoes, or they may slip off. You cannot walk safely in untied shoes, and you might trip over your own laces.
- **Apron strings** must be tied and then tucked under the apron top so that they cannot dangle over flames and catch fire.
- **Wet uniform** must always be changed for a dry one. As well as making you feel uncomfortable, and therefore more likely to make a mistake, a wet uniform does not protect you as well.
- **Loose clothing** is a hazard as it might get caught on a table or cooker, causing you to stumble. If you are carrying anything hot or sharp, you could injure yourself or a colleague. It might also catch fire as you lean over a gas flame.

Manual handling

You might be asked to lift or move objects that may be heavy or large. The items may be at varying temperatures, from freezing to boiling, and some items could be damp or greasy. All of these could cause injury if not handled properly.

The main injuries that can occur from manual handling are:

- back and spinal injuries
- muscular injuries
- fractures
- sprains
- cuts, bruises and burns.

Avoiding injury from lifting and carrying

- Consider whether the item could be split into smaller packages, such as unloading tins from an outer cardboard case.
- Can you shorten the distance the item has to be moved?
- Can someone help you with this, as it might be safer with two people?
- Can you use a trolley or sack truck? Do not load a trolley too high because you will not be able to see what is in front of you and the load may fall off.
- Consider where you are taking the items. – are there any uneven floors, stairs, high or low temperatures or low lighting? These will all make a difference.
- Avoid handling wet or greasy loads, and do not try to move items when floors are wet or slippery.
- Wear the correct PPE, for example a padded jacket and gloves when working in walk-in fridges and freezers.

- Do not unload, carry or store heavy items, sharp items or hot items above shoulder height.
- If you are lifting, unloading or moving heavy items as a regular part of your job, you should receive manual handling training.
- If you are not sure, or do not feel able to move something, then do not move it. Once you have damaged your back it could be damaged forever.

Correct lifting technique

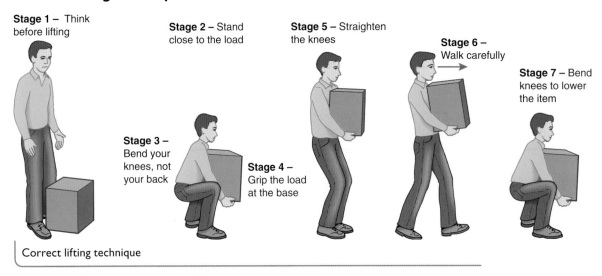

Correct lifting technique

1 Assess the load – can it be made smaller? Can lifting or carrying equipment be used? Consider the weight and shape of the item, and where you need to move it to.
2 Stand close to the load with feet apart and your weight evenly spread; your chin should be tucked in and your shoulders level.
3 Bend your knees, keeping your back straight, and grip the load at the base or with handles, keeping it close to your body.
4 Bring the load up to waist height and straighten your knees.
5 Walk carefully, making sure that you can see where you are going.
6 Lower the item with bent knees and straight back.

> ### Activity
>
> 1 What are the risks of wearing loose clothing in the workplace?
> 2 When using machinery, what could cause someone to get entangled or entrapped in it?
> 3 What items should you be particularly careful of lifting or moving?
> 4 Which part of your body is most at risk of serious damage when lifting or moving items?
> 5 If you were asked to put away a large delivery of frozen food, what are the four safety precautions you should take?

Electricity

Hospitality firms use a wide range of electrical equipment and it must be used with care to avoid accidents and injury. Under the Electricity at Work Regulations (1989) all portable electrical equipment must be tested for safety by a qualified electrician (this is called PAT testing). They will also check that cables and flexes are in good working order and are not damaged, and that the correct fuses are being used. **Circuit breakers** must also be checked regularly.

If you notice any damaged or faulty electrical equipment, do not use it. Warn others and report it to a supervisor or manager. If a person comes into direct contact with an electrical current, an electric shock can occur, which can be serious or even fatal.

Faulty electrical equipment can also cause fires and may result in burns.

If someone you are working with has an electric shock:
- switch off the electricity
- raise the alarm
- call for medical help or first aid.

If it is not possible to switch the electricity off, free the person from it, protecting yourself using something like a thick, dry oven cloth or something made from wood or rubber – the electricity will not conduct through these. Do not touch the person directly or the electricity will be transmitted to you.

Activity

  1 Suggest two problems with electrical equipment you would need to report to a supervisor or manager.
  2 What should you do if you think someone has experienced an electric shock? What must you **not** do?
  3 What is PAT testing?

Stretch yourself

Find out where the RCD or circuit breaker is at work/college for each piece of electrical equipment.

Fire and explosion

Fire and possible explosions are always risks that need to be considered in hospitality premises. The possible causes of fire and explosion are:

- gas jets or open flames
- overheated oils and other hot liquid substances and **fuel gels**
- electrical faults or faulty equipment
- gas leaks or gas build-up
- chemicals
- carelessness and misuse of equipment
- smoking.

Smoking is not allowed in most buildings. Do not smoke outside near gas canisters, waste oil or items such as paper and cardboard.

The Regulatory Reform (Fire Safety) Order, which came into force in 2006, applies to England and Wales (Scotland and Northern Ireland have similar laws). These laws put the responsibility for fire safety on to the employer or business owner. They must conduct a risk assessment of the premises and business, identify the risks and put measures in place to make them as safe as possible. This may include:

- having fire alarms and testing them regularly to make sure they are working
- making sure that escape routes are clearly marked and that there are no obstacles in the way
- ensuring that fire detection systems are in place
- providing suitable equipment for extinguishing fires.

Three elements are needed for fire – heat, oxygen and fuel. If one of these is taken away the fire will not start or continue. Extinguishing fires relies on removing one of these elements, such as restricting the supply of oxygen (a foam extinguisher acts in this way), or removing the heat (a water extinguisher cools down the burning material).

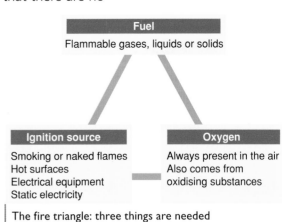

The fire triangle: three things are needed

Training in procedures to follow in case of fire or other emergencies is essential for all staff. There must be a fire and evacuation plan in place. Staff must know how to follow the plan and **evacuate** the building safely, assisting customers and visitors where appropriate.

Fire extinguishers are a very important part of fire safety and there are different types for use on various kinds of fire. Only use an extinguisher if it is safe for you to do so and if you have been trained in its use.

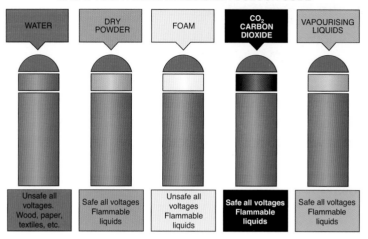

Types of fire extinguishers and their uses

If a fire breaks out in your work area:

- raise the alarm and warn others verbally
- turn off gas supplies using a central cut-off point if possible
- never put yourself in danger; only tackle small fires and only if you have been trained to do so. If in doubt – get out!
- leave by the appointed escape route and go to the assembly point; remain there and do not re-enter the building until told that you may do so.

Key words

Fuel gels – flammable gels often used to heat food service equipment.

Evacuate – leave the building.

Circuit breaker – a device that cuts the electrical current in a split second to protect people.

Activity

1 Name four ways that an accidental fire could start in a kitchen.
2 What are the three elements needed for a fire to start?
3 What type of fire extinguisher would you use on a chip-pan fire?

Stretch yourself

Draw up an evacuation route for your home in case the kitchen caught fire.

First aid

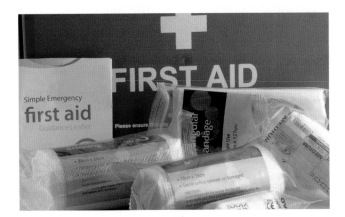

All firms must have a first aid box available for staff to use, and most will have a registered first aider. You will normally find the first aid box in the kitchen, as it must be available for all staff when at work. Do not have it locked away in the stores or the chef's office.

Typical first aid box contents will include:

- a range of blue plasters
- eye wash
- a range of wound dressings
- a triangular bandage
- safety pins
- disposable gloves.

You need to know who the registered **first aider** is and how to contact them. This person will normally have had training from an organisation such as St John's Ambulance and will be able to help with minor injuries. They may also be the person who will call an ambulance if needed.

In an emergency do not hesitate to call 999 yourself. It is better to be safe than sorry, and a wasted ambulance trip is better than a dead or seriously injured colleague.

Activity

1 What colour are first aid plasters in a kitchen and why?
2 What other safety factor do special plasters have?

Stretch yourself

Find out about becoming a qualified first aider at work, including how much it costs and how long it takes.

Key words

First aider – someone qualified to give first aid.

Security procedures

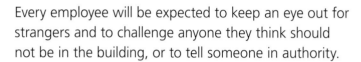

Businesses may also experience some external dangers, hazards and threats, and there will be some planned **security procedures** to deal with these. For example, most firms have a security check on who can enter the building through the staff entrance. This might be through door **access codes**, employing security staff or using CCTV to monitor the building. You must never give out any security door codes or lend your pass to someone else.

Every employee will be expected to keep an eye out for strangers and to challenge anyone they think should not be in the building, or to tell someone in authority.

It is unlikely that a hotel in the UK will be a terrorist target, but sometimes its guests can be. If you see any packages or parcels you do not recognise, or see something unusual, always report it. It might just be a parcel that a guest has left behind, but it could be something more dangerous.

It is normal to have an alarm system switched on after the business has closed, in case anyone tries to break in.

You should know what the security procedures are at work, and who to inform if you spot anything suspicious.

Activity

1 Explain carefully what you would do if you saw a parcel left behind in the restaurant.
2 What would you do if someone asked you for the staff door access code?

Your responsibility

This chapter has covered some of the times when you will need to report issues to your supervisor, but if you see anything that affects the safety, hygiene or security of the business, you must report it. If you do not and someone gets injured, you might be prosecuted and you will certainly wish that you had said something.

Stretch yourself

Produce a booklet to give to new staff on maintaining a safe, hygienic and secure workplace.

Key words

Access code – security code used by staff to open doors.

Security procedures – normal actions carried out by a business to keep it safe and secure.

Chapter 9   Teamwork

Learning objectives

By the end of this chapter you should:
- Know how to plan and organise your own work
- Know how to work effectively with other team members
- Know how to further develop your own skills

This chapter concentrates being an effective member of the team at work, and on developing your own skills.

Planning and organising your own work

Working in the hospitality industry is very time dependent. Food needs to be prepared, cooked and served on time to the customers. As part of a team it is important that you know what your role is at work, and how you fit into the bigger picture.

Arriving on time

The first task you need to manage is to get to work on time every day, and be ready in the kitchen just before your shift is due to start. If you start work at 08:00, be there by 07:55 in your clean whites and you will be seen as an organised member of the team; get there at 08:05 and you will be seen as an unreliable person who cannot organise their own life.

Following instructions and asking for help

Once you are at work you will be expected to be able to work on your own, without constant supervision.

First, you will be given instructions on what to do. These may vary from day to day, or may be the same tasks each day. When you are told what to do it

is a good idea to repeat this back to your supervisor, so they know that you have understood what you have to do.

If you do not understand or are unsure about what you are being asked to do, then always ask for help and advice. This will help you to develop your own skills and will ensure that you do the work to the correct standard, and do not waste food or damage equipment. Write notes if will help you to do the job properly.

Remember, your supervisor is there to help you and show you what to do. Many firms will have set ways of doing tasks, and this is called an **operational procedure**.

Prioritising tasks

One of the keys to planning your work is to ensure that everything is completed on time and to the correct standard.

As it is likely that you will have a list of jobs to do, you will have to decide which ones to do first and which ones can be left till later. This is called **prioritising** your work. As a guide, anything that is needed for the next service time is done first. Check to see how long some tasks will take and work backwards to find the start time.

For example, if a recipe requires an hour in the oven and service is at 12:30, then it must be in the oven by 11:20 to ensure that it is ready to serve by 12:30. If the preparation time is 30 minutes then you have to start work on this by 10:50.

While the dish is cooking you can get on with your other tasks, such as preparing the garnish.

Keeping everything you need organised and available

Mise-en-place

This French phrase means having everything in place before you start. In a kitchen it means having items ready before you need to use them. So, before service a chef will have prepared the meat items and have them in a fridge, the garnishes will be prepared and stored ready to use, basic sauces will be cooked, salads made up and vegetables prepared. This means that when service comes they can finish off the dishes quickly and customers do not have to wait long.

Using recipes

- Read the recipe through twice – if anything is not clear, ask for help.
- Prepare your mise-en-place. This means assembling the ingredients and equipment you will need to make the dish. Weigh out the ingredients and have them in separate bowls, and clear your work area. If an ingredient or a piece of equipment is not available you need to find out before you start cooking, so that you can arrange a substitute or make another dish.
- See if the recipe requires an oven to be preheated and, if so, make sure you set the oven in time for it to get hot.
- Always follow a recipe exactly. If you do not, then the dish will not be as it should be and it might have to be thrown away, wasting food and time.
- Always check on food while it is cooking, as different ovens will cook food differently. You must avoid burning the food or presenting undercooked food for service. Part of the skill of a chef is in knowing how to work with different ovens and adjusting cooking time or temperature accordingly.
- If the recipe has a picture of the finished dish, then present your food exactly like the picture.

Work in a clean and tidy way

There are several reasons why you should always work tidily. One of the main ones is that, by doing so, you will minimise the risk of cross-contamination or food poisoning. You have a legal responsibility not to cause food poisoning so you must clean as you go.

- Always clean the work surface before you start.
- Dispose of rubbish as you go, putting food waste in the correct bin (many firms arrange for this to be taken away and used for making compost). Put other waste in the right bins, recycling as much as you can, keeping glass and other recyclable items separate.
- Remember that some food items, which might be seen as waste from the recipe you are producing, can be used in other ways in the kitchen and must not be thrown away. If in doubt, ask your supervisor.

- Put food that is not for immediate use in the fridge as soon as possible, in a container labelled with the contents, date it was put in the fridge and use-by date.
- Carry on cleaning the work surface and chopping boards as you go.
- Wash up equipment and put it back in the right place so that other staff can find it when they need it.
- Check as you go that you are following the recipe properly and, if anything goes wrong, ask for help. If you do make a mistake chefs with more experience than you may know how to save the recipe and avoid wasting the food.

Activity

1 If your bus or train to work was late and you knew you were going to be 30 minutes late for work, what should you do?
2 Why is it very important for chefs and other hospitality staff to arrive at work on time?
3 What are the qualities that make you a good employee?
4 Why do chefs need to manage their time well?
5 Why is good time management crucial when working in the hospitality industry?
6 Give three reasons why you should work tidily.
7 Give two reasons why mise-en-place is important.

Working effectively with team members

To be a good employee of a business you need to be able to work in a team. No matter how good you are as a chef, if you are not a team player you will not be a success at work. A sign of a good team is that all the members will support each other to get the result they need.

A good team member is always punctual for work and does not take time off unless they are genuinely sick and should not be in work. Someone who takes odd days off soon loses the support of their colleagues, and it can lead

to them losing their job. If you are going to be off, let your employer know as soon as you can so that the other members of staff can rearrange the work to cover you.

This also means that if one of your colleagues is off sick you will help out to cover their work, and possibly do some extra hours at work. You might be asked to change your shift to cover for someone else – try to do this even if it means that you will have to rearrange your social life. A good team member will always work to ensure the that customers' needs are met.

However, it is very important that you do not try to help your colleagues so much that your own work suffers. Your first priority has to be to get your own work done, and then help others if you have time.

You are not only part of the kitchen team; you are part of a much larger team. A successful hospitality business may have many teams including reception, bars, food service, kitchens, maintenance, housekeeping and porters. All of these departments need to work together as a wider team to ensure an efficient workflow and to meet employer and customer expectations. Because of this you must never blame another department in front of the customer; sometimes you may have to 'take one for the team'.

What makes a good team?

Good teams are generally more effective and creative. There are a number of factors that contribute to a good team:

- Good communication.
- Commitment from each member of the team – colleagues will expect you to play your part in the team as your performance will have an effect on the performance of the whole team. It is important that every member of the team performs to their best so as not to let the team down.
- Team members are all punctual.
- Team members are all reliable.
- Team members are all flexible.
- Team members support one another.
- All team members work together to achieve the aims and objectives of the organisation.
- All team members understand the tasks that have to be achieved in the set time.
- All team members are able to work with deadlines and are able to achieve the targets set.
- The team has good leadership.

Communication skills

This is a key part of a good team. If you watch a sports team in action they are always communicating with each other so that they can react to changing

circumstances; a team at work should do the same. You may need to pass on important information to your team members or receive important information from them.

Speaking

Always speak clearly, with good pronunciation and sufficient volume. Check whether the person can hear and understand what you are saying. Try not to speak too fast, especially when speaking with someone whose first language is not English. Show interest when you are speaking to other people and respond appropriately to questions they may ask you.

Listening

Listening is very important, sometimes more important than speaking. Good listeners:

- avoid any distractions
- concentrate on what is being said
- think about what is being said
- show interest in the person speaking and do not look bored
- maintain eye contact with the person talking and acknowledge what is being said
- if necessary, ask questions to confirm what is being said
- clarify what has been said in their own words.

Writing and reading

Written communication may be used when:

- dealing with food or drinks orders, including specific customer requests
- following or adapting recipes
- ordering food or equipment
- following instructions on food products, equipment or cleaning chemicals
- reading instructions or leaving instructions for others.

Using good speaking and listening skills in the kitchen

It is important that you write clearly so that others understand your meaning. When reading what someone else has written, ask for clarification if you do not understand it.

Dealing with problems in the team

Sometimes teams do not work as well as they should, and this is usually because two members have a problem with each other. This could be due to a disagreement over how to do something, one of them thinking the other has let them down, or just because they support different sports teams.

If you are having a problem with someone in the team there are several actions you can take.

First, you can talk to the person concerned, one-to-one, away from anybody else. Explain quietly to them what you think the problem is and how you think it can be sorted out. For this to be successful, try not to blame the other person – it might be partly your fault as well.

It is surprising how often such a direct approach works, as the person concerned may not be aware of the problem, and between the pair of you a solution can be found.

If you do not feel able to do this, or you think the person is deliberately picking on you, talk to your supervisor. Ask to talk to them after service and explain what the problem is. They may have a suggestion on how you can resolve it, or they may need to speak to the other person. Sometimes they will have a meeting with you both to resolve the problem.

Most solutions will require both people to give a bit, as it is unlikely that anyone is 100 per cent right. Once the problem has been discussed and resolved, it is important to still keep working on the relationship and to develop a positive relationship with the other person. It doesn't mean you have to be best friends, but you do have to work together for the benefit of the team and, ultimately, the customer.

Activity

1 What are the advantages to you of being a good employee and team member?
2 List three things that will make a good team at work.
3 What is meant by good communication?
4 Suggest what may happen if members of a kitchen team do not communicate with each other.
5 What makes a good listener?
6 When writing down a customer's order, why is important to write clearly?
7 How would you try to improve a poor working relationship?

Developing your own skills

In order to develop your own skills you must know what your skills are, and in particular what skills you need to improve to reach the required standard.

Identifying areas for improvement

We all make mistakes, but as long as we learn from them we are improving.

You will know what you need to improve by:

■ your own analysis of your work and by comparing your finished dish with the photo you are working from
■ comparing your dish with others in your class
■ tasting your cooking and seeing if it tastes good
■ comparing your own knife skills with others, to see how skilful you are; a **skilled** worker is one who can produce the required standard of work in a reasonable amount of time – skilled workers work quickly
■ asking your colleagues and supervisor for feedback.

Seeking feedback

You will get feedback from:

■ your supervisor, who will be observing what you do
■ your colleagues, who will comment on your work whether you like it or not
■ customers, who may send comments back to the kitchen.

Whenever you realise that you are not working to the required standard, or when you receive feedback from others who tell you this, you have to turn this to your advantage.

You can do this by:

1 asking exactly where the dish/skill is not up to standard
2 asking how you can improve it, and where you can see an example of the required standard
3 asking to be shown what to do by someone who has the skills you need.

One chef's favourite phrase to students was, 'load of rubbish, no marks, in the bin'. This is not useful feedback as it does not tell the students how to improve. If you ever receive this kind of feedback you must ask for more explanation of how to improve.

Of course, when you are told how to improve your work, do follow what you are told.

Agreeing a learning plan

As you are working towards a qualification you must know what you have to do to gain the qualification. You might be using a logbook, which records when you achieve the required skills, but you should also be working to a **learning plan**, which shows when you will be learning each skill or set of skills. This will help you to plan your time and enable you to see if you are on target.

Your learning plan is personal to you and has to be regularly updated and changed to show how well you are doing. For example, you might have a date set to achieve a specific skill but you achieve it early, so you should change your plan and go on to the next target. Or you might take a bit longer to master a skill, so you should put back the start date of the next stage in the plan to show when you will be ready to go on to it.

Your learning plan might be electronic or paper-based but it will include a set of skills that you have to achieve within a specific period of time. Larger targets may be split into smaller sections so you can achieve each section and eventually achieve the main goal. Each unit in a qualification will be broken down into the separate **learning outcomes** or **goals**.

Each learning outcome or goal will have a skill you will achieve by a certain date.

Each skill will be linked to one or more **resources** and with **evidence**. Resources are anything that you will use to achieve the goal, and will include food, equipment and books, as well as your lecturer or tutor. Evidence is used to demonstrate that an action has been taken, that progress towards the goal has been made and, finally, that the goal has been achieved.

Your learning plan will be most effective if you review it and update it regularly, at least once week, or after each session.

Stretch yourself

1   Using Recipe 28, brown lamb or mutton stew, in Chapter 4:
    (a) List what you would do for mise-en-place.
    (b) Produce a detailed time plan for a service time of 13:00.
    (c) Describe what would you do if you have found some time when you are doing nothing for the recipe.
2   A new member of staff has joined where you work. How would you help them to be an effective member of the team?
3   See what skills you use at work which are also part of this qualification; arrange for your supervisor to give you a witness statement for your learning log.

Chapter 10 Food safety

Learning objectives

By the end of this chapter you will:
- Know how to keep yourself clean and hygienic
- Know how to keep the working area clean and hygienic
- Know how to store food safely
- Know how to prepare, cook and hold food safely
- Know how to maintain food safety

Why are we so concerned about food safety?

Eating contaminated food can result in **food poisoning**, causing harm, illness and, in some cases, even death. The number of reported cases of food poisoning each year remains too high and, as a large number of food poisoning cases are never reported, no one knows the actual number.

Food poisoning is usually caused by eating food that has become contaminated with bacteria or the toxins they may produce. Sometimes it can be caused by eating foods such as poisonous mushrooms or chemicals that may have got into food, or by organisms such as viruses.

The main symptoms of food poisoning are:
- nausea
- vomiting
- diarrhoea
- dehydration
- sometimes fever and headache.

Risk assessment

Kitchen staff are often the first to become aware of possible **hazards**. If you see one, report it immediately to your supervisor, head chef or line manager.

It is important to assess these hazards and put measures in place to reduce the risk of them occurring. Under the Food Hygiene Regulations 2006 all businesses must have a **food safety** management system and keep the necessary records to support it.

Hazard Analysis Critical Control Point (HACCP)

This food safety management system can be used to help identify any potential hazards, and then to identify the critical control points or stages in any food process where hazards could occur. Once the hazards have been identified, measures are put in place to control them and keep the food safe.

The HACCP system has seven stages:
1   Identify hazards – what could go wrong?
2   Identify Critical Control Points (CCPs). These are the important stages where things could go wrong.
3   Set critical limits for each **CCP** – for example, temperature requirements on delivery of fresh chicken.
4   Monitor CCPs and put checks in place to stop problems happening.
5   Corrective action – what will be done if something goes wrong?
6   Verification – check that the HACCP plan is working.
7   Documentation – record all of the above.

The system must be updated regularly, especially when new items are introduced to the menu or systems change (for example, a new piece of cooking equipment is used). New controls must be put in place to include them.

Keeping the records that support this system is very important for **due diligence**. Records prove that you have completed the necessary procedures to ensure food safety. Records may include staff training records, fridge and freezer temperature records, records of reported staff illness, lists of suppliers, calibration of temperature probes and many more relevant records.

Legal responsibilities

The law and food business operators

All food businesses must:
- be registered with the local authority
- cooperate with the Environmental Health Officer/Environmental Health Practitioner (**EHO/EHP**)
- put proper food safety practices in place.

An EHO/EHP is employed by local authorities to oversee the standards of food safety in their area. They can enter any food premises at any reasonable time to inspect them. They can advise, serve notices for improvement and, in extreme cases, inform the courts to take legal action resulting in fines or even the closure of food premises and imprisonment.

The law and food handlers

Individual food handlers also have legal responsibilities. This includes anyone working in the catering business. It is a **legal requirement** that they:
- receive food safety training relevant to the work they are doing, so that they understand the principles of food safety and how to avoid food poisoning
- work in a way that does not endanger or contaminate food, and not serve food that they know is contaminated
- report anything that may have an effect on food safety, such as a fridge running at the wrong temperature, and cooperate with the food safety measures that the employer has put in place
- report any illness, especially if stomach related, to a supervisor before starting work; after suffering such an illness they must not return to work until 48 hours after the last symptom.

> **Professional tip**
>
> For further information about food safety matters, speak to your line manager, an EHO/EHP, or look at your local authority food safety websites. Also try the Food Standards Agency, www.food.gov.uk; the Chartered Institute of Environmental Health (CIEH), www.cieh.org; and Highfield, www.highfield.co.uk.

> **Activity**
>
> 1. What are three advantages of a business having good standards of food safety?
> 2. What is food poisoning and what are the main symptoms?
> 3. Suggest three possible food safety hazards in a kitchen.
> 4. What must a food handler do if they arrive at work feeling unwell?
> 5. Suggest some of the ways that a food handler can help to achieve high standards of food safety.

> **Key words**
>
> **Hazard** – anything with the potential to cause harm.
>
> **Food safety** – putting measures in place to ensure food is safe to eat and will not cause illness.
>
> **Hazard analysis** – identifying all the possible hazards and putting measures in place to prevent them from causing harm.
>
> **CCP** – Critical Control Point; a point at which something could go wrong and where a control measure could be put in place to keep the hazard under control.
>
> **Due diligence** – proving that you have completed the necessary procedures to ensure food safety.
>
> **EHO/EHP** – Environmental Health Officer/Environmental Health Practitioner; employed by local authorities to ensure that the required standards of food safety are met. Also involved with health and safety.
>
> **Legal requirement** – something that must be done by law.

Stretch yourself

If you have a part-time job, write a report that describes how your employer ensures food safety.

Personal appearance

As a chef you must always look clean and professional. You need to practise a high level of personal hygiene. The protective clothing you wear at work must be clean, hygienic and not damaged.

The chef's uniform

Wearing clean, hygienic kitchen clothing is a legal requirement when you work with food. Your uniform will protect you from hot liquids and other dangers that you may come into contact with in the kitchen. You will need a clean uniform every day and must change it if it gets dirty or stained. Clean clothing is important to prevent the transfer of bacteria from dirty clothing to food.

A clean uniform also promotes a professional image; it gives a visible sign of cleanliness and good hygiene standards. It will show a positive impression to customers and visitors, giving them confidence in the establishment.

Key words

Dermatitis – inflammation of the skin that can make it red, itchy and scaly. It can be caused by contact with chemicals or with some foodstuffs.

Chef's jacket

These jackets are designed as hygienic work wear, as well as to protect the chef in the kitchen. They are usually made from lightweight and comfortable fabrics such as cotton, a coated cotton or polyester-cotton. White is still the preferred colour because dirt and stains will be visible and white withstands hot laundry well.

Your jacket should fit well and not be too tight. You should be able to move easily so that if, for example, hot liquid is spilled on it, you can pull it away from your skin easily to prevent burning.

It is safer to wear jackets with long sleeves as these protect your arms from splashed hot liquids or fats to reduce the risk of burns and scalds; they will also protect you from possible contact **dermatitis.**

Remember to change your chefs' jacket daily and more frequently if dirty or stained.

Chef's trousers

These were traditionally blue-and-white check but now a variety of colours and designs are available. Like jackets, cotton, cotton mixtures or coated cotton are the preferred fabrics. They should be loose fitting so that they are comfortable and can be pulled away from the skin easily to prevent burning if hot liquid is spilled on them.

Chef's jacket and trousers

Chef's apron

Aprons also come in a variety of fabrics and styles – they can be a full 'bib' apron or tie at the waist. Your apron should come to just below your knees and be wide enough to wrap around the body; the ties are crossed over then tied at the front. This offers maximum protection from spilt hot liquids and oil, and the ties at the front mean it can be removed quickly if necessary.

Sometimes different colours of apron are used for different purposes. For example, butchers' aprons are blue-and-white striped. They can also be used to separate different kitchen tasks, such as raw preparation and cooked food. Remember to change your apron regularly, especially if dirty or stained.

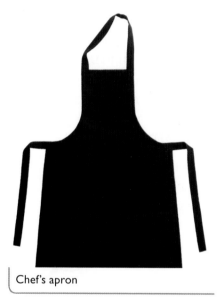

Chef's apron

Chef's or cook's hat

The tall chef's hat (**toque**) is a traditional item and often shows the status of a chef. **Skullcaps** are now used in many modern kitchens because they are more comfortable, cheaper and easier to wash. A wide variety of colours are available so chefs' **status** or sections being worked in can be shown by different coloured skullcaps.

Chef's hat

The main purpose of a hat is to prevent loose hair getting into the food. Where the hair is longer than collar length, a hairnet should be worn under the hat. Disposable hats are now available and come in a variety of styles.

Neckties

Traditionally, kitchens have been very hot places and chefs have worn a necktie to mop perspiration from their brow. With improved ventilation systems they are no longer essential and, with some modern styles of chef's jackets, neckties are not appropriate. They are available in a wide range of colours so, like the hats, can be used to show status or section.

Safety shoes

There are many different varieties of **safety shoes**. They must be sturdy, with reinforced toecaps that protect the feet from falling heavy or sharp objects and from hot liquids. Shoes should be the correct size, comfortable and offer good support because chefs spend a long time on their feet; they must also be kept clean. Open-toed shoes or trainers must not be worn in the kitchen; they would not protect the feet from hot, heavy or sharp items.

Safety shoes

Disposable gloves

Sometimes it is good practice to wear disposable gloves when preparing food. This may be to prevent strong food smells from staying on your hands, such as fish and onions. They can also be used for high-risk foods; for example, if you are plating up food for service which requires you to use your hands rather than a utensil, it is a good precaution to wear disposable gloves. These will help prevent transferring bacteria from your hands to the food.

Care and maintenance of your uniform

Kitchen uniform needs proper care and must be repaired or replaced when necessary. It must be well laundered and ironed, kept in good condition and repairs carried out as necessary. Shoes must also be kept in good repair, cleaned and polished.

> ### Key words
>
> **Toque** – a traditional tall chef's hat.
>
> **Skullcap** – a close-fitting hat.
>
> **Status** – someone's seniority or position.
>
> **Safety shoes** – strong, enclosed shoes with reinforced toecaps to protect the feet from heavy or sharp objects and hot liquids.

> ### Health and safety
>
> Make sure that your uniform is in good repair. The ends of sleeves can fray and hanging threads could get into food, catch on machinery or catch fire over gas jets.

> ### Activity
>
> 1 A good chef's uniform looks smart and professional. What are the other reasons for wearing it?
> 2 What explanation would you give to others in your kitchen about the importance of wearing a chef's hat? What type of chef's hat would you recommend?
> 3 Why is it important to wear safety shoes in a kitchen and not trainers?
> 4 What are the main reasons for wearing protective clothing in the kitchen

> ### Stretch yourself
>
> Design a poster to go in the staff changing room at work that will remind staff of the correct uniform to wear.

Personal hygiene

Personal hygiene is extremely important when handling food because bacteria can be transferred easily from humans to food.

A daily shower or bath is essential to remove body odour, sweat, dirt and bacteria. Change your underwear daily and use an antiperspirant deodorant.

Hands and nails

- Keep nails short and clean.
- When handling high-risk foods, wear disposable gloves and change these gloves for each task.
- Always cover any cuts with a blue waterproof dressing (plaster) then wash hands thoroughly.

Hand washing

Contamination from hands can happen very easily and could result in harmful bacteria being passed on to food. Great care must be taken with hand washing to avoid this; thorough hand washing is essential.

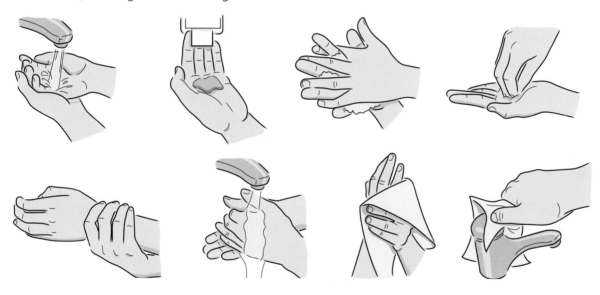

1 Use a basin provided just for hand washing.
2 Wet hands under warm running water.
3 Apply liquid soap.
4 Rub hands together, including between fingers and thumbs.
5 Remember fingertips, nails and wrists. (If a nailbrush is used, make sure it is clean and disinfected.)
6 Rinse off under running water.
7 Dry hands on a paper towel; use the paper towel to turn the tap off then dispose of it into a foot-operated waste bin.

Hands should be washed:

- when you enter the kitchen, before starting work and handling any food
- after a break
- after using the toilet
- after smoking or eating
- between different tasks, but especially after handling raw food and before handling cooked/high-risk food
- if you touch your hair, nose or mouth/face
- after coughing/sneezing and nose blowing
- after you apply or change a dressing on a cut or burn
- after using cleaning materials, cleaning preparation areas, equipment or contaminated surfaces
- after handling kitchen waste, external food packaging, money or flowers.

Health and safety

Blue dressings are used because they are easy to detect if they fall into food. They can also be identified by metal detectors used by food manufacturers because they contain a narrow metal strip.

Jewellery and cosmetics

- Do not wear jewellery or watches in the kitchen. These items trap bacteria that could contaminate food; the items themselves may fall into food and could also become caught in machinery and cause injury.
- Avoid the use of perfumes and aftershaves when working with food, and cosmetics should only be used vary sparingly.

Health and safety

Strong smelling items such as perfume and aftershave, and even strong smelling deodorants, can taint the food being handled so should not be used by food handlers. In a hot kitchen cosmetics can flake and could fall into food; they also stop the cooling processes of the skin from working properly.

Hair

Hair can be both a physical and bacterial contaminant if it gets into food. It can also be the cause of customer complaints and possible loss of custom.

- Hair must be washed regularly and kept clean and tidy.
- Your hair must be short or tied back neatly. Wear a suitable kitchen hat that stops hair from getting into food. If hair is longer than collar length, wear a net under the hat.
- Men should be clean shaven or wear a beard net.

> **Professional tip**
>
> It is not a legal requirement for chefs to wear a hat but it is strongly recommended that they do so.

Dental hygiene

It is important to look after your teeth and mouth as part of good grooming, as well as to maintain good health.

- Clean your teeth at least twice a day and use a mouthwash.
- Visit your dentist regularly.
- Do not touch your mouth when handling food.

Feet

Chefs and others working in the hospitality industry are likely to be on their feet for much of the day, so take care of your feet. Make sure they are dried thoroughly after a bath or shower and keep toenails neatly cut. Wear clean, well-fitting, absorbent socks and proper, well-fitting kitchen shoes (see above).

Poor hygiene and practices – what to avoid

- Generally you should not eat or drink in food production areas during working times, unless tasting food to ensure quality and check seasoning. Drinking water is permitted and encouraged – some establishments provide water coolers for staff use.
- Never wear your uniform outside the kitchen premises as bacteria can be carried from the outside on your uniform into the kitchen where it can then get into food.
- Do not chew gum while in uniform and in the kitchen. It looks very unprofessional and will prevent you from tasting the food properly.
- Do not touch your face, hair, nose or mouth as this can transfer bacteria to the food.
- Smoking is not allowed in public areas. It is also unhygienic as the fingers touch the lips and can transfer bacteria on to food. If chefs smoke during their break period outside, they must not be in uniform and must wash their hands thoroughly on their return to the kitchen.

- Make sure you wash your hands regularly and thoroughly. Irregular and incorrect hand washing can cause cross-contamination.

Personal illnesses

Report any illness to your supervisor as soon as possible and before handling any food. This is a legal requirement and includes:

- diarrhoea and/or vomiting, nausea and stomach pain; this may well be food poisoning
- infected (septic) cuts, burns or spots
- eye or ear infections
- cold or flu symptoms, including sore throat
- skin problems such as dermatitis.

Also report any illnesses you had when on holiday and family members or friends you have had contact with who have the above symptoms, especially where they are stomach related.

Cuts and wounds

Any infected (**septic**) cuts and wounds should be reported to a supervisor. Wash, dry then cover any cuts, burns or grazes with a blue waterproof dressing, then wash your hands.

Key words

Septic – cuts, burns and so on infected with **pathogenic bacteria**; they are often wet with a white or yellow appearance.

Pathogenic bacteria – microorganisms that could multiply in food and cause food poisoning.

Activity

1 Why should chefs not wear their kitchen uniform when going outside for a break?
2 Why do so many kitchens use disposable kitchen paper rather than cloths now?
3 Suggest five personal hygiene rules you would include in a kitchen poster for staff information.
4 What do the letters HACCP stand for and how is this used?
5 Why should jewellery and watches not be worn in the kitchen?
6 What is the correct procedure to follow if you cut your finger while working?

Keeping work areas clean and hygienic

It is a legal requirement that food areas are kept clean and hygienic, and that food premises are designed with good food safety in mind.

Controlling cross-contamination

Cross-contamination is when bacteria or other contaminants are transferred from contaminated food (often raw food) to ready-to-eat food. It is a cause of food poisoning and care must be taken to avoid it. Causes of cross-contamination include:

■ foods touching, for example raw and cooked meat
■ raw meat or poultry dripping on to high-risk foods
■ soil from dirty vegetables coming into contact with high-risk foods
■ dirty cloths or dirty equipment
■ equipment used for raw then cooked food without proper cleaning/ disinfection, such as chopping boards or knives
■ hands touching raw then cooked food, not washing hands thoroughly between tasks and so on.

Having separate areas for different foods, storage, processes and service will help to reduce the risk of contamination and assist efficient working and effective cleaning. A linear workflow in food production areas should also be in place:

1 delivery
2 storage
3 preparation
4 cooking
5 hot holding
6 serving.

This means there will be no crossover of activities that could result in cross-contamination.

'Dirty areas', or **high-risk areas**, that involve preparation or storage of raw foods, or cleaning of items such as dirty vegetables, need to be kept separate from the 'clean areas', or **low-risk areas**, where cold preparations, finishing and serving takes place.

Separate areas for raw and high-risk foods are always recommended and, if this is not possible, keep them well away from each other, making sure that working areas are thoroughly cleaned and disinfected between tasks.

Work area and equipment

■ Kitchen surfaces and equipment should be installed to allow for efficient cleaning and **disinfection**.

- Equipment and surfaces need to be smooth, impervious (not absorb liquids) and must, of course, be **non-corrosive**, non-toxic and must not crack, chip or flake.
- Many kitchens have a 'no glass' policy to prevent the possibility of broken glass getting into food.

Table 10.1 provides examples of the types of materials used and requirements of work areas.

Table 10.1 Requirements of work areas

Lighting	Must be bright enough for tasks to be completed safely and without eye strain, and allow cleaning to be carried out efficiently.
Ventilation	Using canopies over essential areas prevents excessive heat, condensation, circulation of air-borne contaminants, grease vapours and odours, and gives a more comfortable working environment.
Floors	Need to be hard wearing and in good condition; they must be impervious, non-slip and easy to keep clean. Edges between floor and walls should be coved (curved) to prevent dirt collecting in corners.
Walls	Need to be non-porous, smooth, easy to clean and light in colour. Suitable wall coverings are plastic cladding and stainless steel sheeting.
Ceilings	Ceiling finishes must resist build-up of condensation, which could encourage mould. They should be of a non-flaking material and be washable. Non-porous ceiling panels and tiles are often used; non-flaking paints are also useful.
Drainage	Drainage must be adequate for the work being completed without causing flooding. If channels, grease traps and gullies are used, they should allow for frequent cleaning.
Windows/doors	These provide possibilities for pests to enter the building so should fit well into the frames with no gaps. They should be fitted with screening; strip-curtains and doors should have metal kick plates.

Colour-coded equipment

Worktops and chopping boards come into contact with the food you prepare, so need special attention. Make sure that chopping boards are in good condition; cracks and splits could hold on to bacteria and this could be transferred to food. Colour-coded chopping boards are a good way to keep different types of food separate.

Professional tip

As well as colour-coded chopping boards, some kitchens also provide colour-coded knives, cloths, cleaning equipment, storage trays, bowls and even staff uniforms to help prevent cross-contamination.

Colour-coded chopping boards

Kitchen cloths

Kitchen cloths are a perfect growing area for bacteria. Different cloths for different areas will help to reduce cross-contamination, and it is especially important to use different cloths for raw food and cooked food preparation. Use of disposable cloths or kitchen towels is the most hygienic way to clean food areas.

Use tea towels with great care as they can easily spread bacteria. Do not use them as an all-purpose cloth, and do not keep them on your shoulder (the cloth touches the neck and hair, and these can be sources of bacteria).

Maintenance

All food premises, fittings and equipment must be kept in good repair to ensure food safety. Cracked surfaces or chipped equipment could support the multiplication of bacteria, while a fridge running at the wrong temperature may allow bacteria to multiply in food. If you notice anything is damaged, broken or faulty report it to a supervisor immediately. You may have specific reporting forms to do this.

Cleaning and disinfection

Clean food areas play an essential part in the production of safe food and it is a requirement to plan, record and check all cleaning as part of a planned **cleaning schedule**.

As a food handler it is your responsibility, along with those working with you, to keep food areas clean and hygienic at all times. Clean as you go and do not allow waste to build up; clean up any spills straight away.

Some kitchen areas, such as floors and walls, will need planned and thorough cleaning, but some items, especially in high-risk areas and where high-risk foods are handled, need both cleaning and disinfection. These are:

- **all food contact surfaces**, such as chopping boards, bowls, spoons and whisks
- **all hand contact surfaces**, such as fridge handles and door handles
- **cleaning materials and equipment**, such as mops, buckets, cloths and hand-wash basins.

Cleaning products

- **Detergents** – designed to remove grease and dirt and hold them in suspension in water; they do not kill bacteria. Detergent works best with hot water.
- **Disinfectant** – designed to destroy bacteria if used properly. Disinfectants must be left on a cleaned, grease-free surface for the required amount of time to be effective. They work best with cool water.
- **Sanitiser** – cleans and disinfects, and usually comes in spray form. It is very useful for work surfaces and equipment, especially between tasks, and also for hand contact surfaces such as fridge handles.
- **Steriliser** – can be used after cleaning to make a surface or piece of equipment bacteria free.

Cleaning and disinfection of kitchen equipment

Clean and **sanitise** worktops and chopping boards before working on them and do this again after use, paying particular attention when they have been used for raw foods.

Small equipment, such as knives, chopping boards, bowls, spoons and tongs, as well as serving cutlery and crockery, could be a cause of cross-contamination. Wash them well, especially when used for a variety of food and for raw foods.

This small equipment can be cleaned and disinfected very effectively by putting it through a dishwasher. Loose debris is scraped or sprayed off, the machine washes at approximately 55 °C using a detergent then rinses at 82 °C, which disinfects and allows items to air dry quickly.

If a dishwasher cannot be used, a double sink method may be in place. Loose debris is removed, the items are washed thoroughly with detergent and hot water, then rinsed in a second sink in very hot water (82 °C if possible) and allowed to air dry.

Large equipment, such as large mixing machines and ovens, cannot be moved so need to be cleaned where they are. This is called 'clean in place' and each item will have a specific method outlined on the cleaning schedule. Sometimes steam cleaning methods are used, which also disinfects the items.

Cleaning of kitchen surfaces

When cleaning kitchen surfaces, either a four-stage or six-stage cleaning process is recommended, as outlined in Table 10.2.

Table 10.2 Kitchen surface cleaning processes

Four stage	Six stage
Remove debris and loose particles	Remove debris and loose particles
Main clean using hot water and sanitiser	Main clean to remove soiling grease
Rinse using clean hot water and cloth if recommended on instructions	Rinse using clean hot water and cloth to remove detergent
Allow to air dry or use kitchen paper	Apply disinfectant; leave for contact time recommended on the container
	Rinse off the disinfectant if recommended
	Allow to air dry or use kitchen paper

Waste disposal

Kitchen waste should be placed in waste bins with lids (preferably foot operated and lined with a strong bin liner). They need to be kept in good condition, away from direct sunlight. Bins should be emptied regularly to avoid cross-contamination and odour, and always left clean and empty at the end of the day.

Staff in kitchens need to become familiar with the separation of different waste items ready for collection and recycling. This may include bottles, cans, waste food, paper and plastic items.

Pests and pest control

Pests in food premises can be a serious source of contamination and disease; having them near food cannot be allowed and is against the law. Pests in food premises can also lead to:

- legal action
- loss of profit
- closure of the business
- loss of reputation
- poor staff morale
- damage to equipment and wastage of food.

Pests can be attracted to food premises because there is food, warmth, shelter, water and possible nesting materials; all reasonable measures must be put in place to keep them out.

Any suspicion of pests being present must be reported to the supervisor or manager immediately. Pest problems are best dealt with by a recognised pest contractor; they can also complete audits and give advice.

Pests include rats, mice, flies, wasps, cockroaches, ants, weevils, birds, domestic pets and wild cats. Signs of pest invasion include sightings of droppings; unpleasant smells; smear marks; damaged or gnawed packaging and food spillages; pupae, larvae, eggs or cases; and holes in skirting boards, door and window frames or gnawed wires.

Pests can be kept out or dealt with in a number of ways:

- Block entry – make sure there are no holes around pipework; block any gaps and cavities where they could get in; seal all drain covers.
- Damage to the building or fixtures and fittings must be repaired quickly.
- Use window/door screening/netting.
- Check deliveries/packaging for pests.
- Place baits and traps in relevant places.
- Use an electronic fly killer.
- Seal containers and do not leave food out in the open.
- Avoid a build-up of waste in the kitchen.
- Do not keep outside waste too close to the kitchen and ensure that containers are emptied regularly and the area is clean and tidy.
- Arrange for professional and organised pest management control, surveys and reports.

Professional tip

The only pests you can deal with yourself are flying insects with an electronic fly killer. Professional help is needed for all other pests.

Key words

Cross-contamination – when contaminants are moved from one place to another, for example bacteria from raw food being transferred to cooked food.

High-risk areas – areas that could be sources of contamination, for example raw meat preparation areas.

Low-risk areas – areas where clean processes are carried out.

Disinfection – bringing any pathogenic bacteria present to a safe level.

Non-corrosive – not susceptible to action that breaks a material down, such as rusting.

Cleaning schedule – a planned programme of cleaning areas and equipment.

Sanitise – cleaning and disinfecting together with one product.

Pest – a creature that could enter food premises, causing damage and contaminating food.

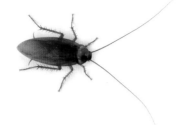

A housefly and a cockroach

Activity

1 Make a poster or checklist for new kitchen staff highlighting ten ways that they can avoid cross-contamination in a kitchen. Include some illustrations.

2 Suggest six kitchen areas or items that should be both **cleaned** and **disinfected**.

3 If you entered the kitchen in the morning and saw small black pellets, chewed packaging and spilled flour, what would you think the problem was and what would you do about it?

4 If you had a number of small kitchen items that you wanted to clean and disinfect, what are the rinse temperatures you would need to achieve to disinfect? How could you do this easily?

5 Which colour-coded chopping board would you use to cut each of the following:
   a raw salmon
   b cooked chicken
   c bread
   d cucumber
   e uncooked carrots
   f raw fillet beef
   g cooked savoury flan?

Storing food safely

Food deliveries

For food to remain in top condition and be safe to eat, correct storage is essential. Only approved suppliers who can assure that food is delivered in the best condition should be used. Food must be delivered in suitable packaging, within the required use-by or best-before dates and at the correct temperature (see Table 10.3).

All deliveries should be checked against the delivery note then moved to the appropriate storage area as soon as possible and within 15 minutes of delivery for chilled/frozen food. Use a food probe to check the temperature of food deliveries: chilled food should be below 5°C; frozen foods should be at or below −18°C. Many suppliers now provide a print-out of temperatures at which the food was delivered.

Dry goods should be in undamaged packaging, well within best-before dates, be completely dry and in perfect condition on delivery.

Storage

Remove food items from outer boxes before placing the products in the fridge, freezer or dry store. Food should be stored with correct labelling so that it is clear what the commodity is. Table 10.3 below gives storage instructions and temperatures for different commodities.

Table 10.3 Storage instructions and temperatures

Food type	Storage temperature	Storage instructions
Refrigerated items in a multi-use fridge	Fridge running at below 5 °C	All food must be covered and labelled with the name of the item and the date.
		Always store raw food at the bottom of the fridge with other items above.
		Keep high-risk foods well away from raw foods.
		Never overload the fridge; to operate properly cold air must be allowed to circulate between items.
		Wrap strong-smelling foods very well as the smell (and taste) can transfer to other foods, e.g. milk.
		Record the temperature at which the fridge is operating. Do this at least once a day and keep the fridge temperatures with other kitchen records.
Frozen foods	Freezer running at −18 °C or below	Separate raw foods from ready-to-eat foods and never allow food to be refrozen once it has defrosted.
		Any food that is to be frozen must be well wrapped or placed in a suitable container with a lid (items may also be vacuum packed).
		Make sure that all food is labelled and dated before freezing.
		Record the temperature at which the freezer is operating. Do this at least once a day and keep the freezer temperatures with other kitchen records.
Raw meat and poultry	Fridges should be running at temperatures between 0 °C and 2 °C	Wherever possible, store in fridges just for meat and poultry to avoid drip contamination. If not already packaged, place on trays, cover well with cling film and label.
		If it is necessary to store meat or poultry in a multi-use fridge, make sure it is covered, labelled and placed at the bottom of the fridge, running below 5 °C, and well away from other items.
Dry goods (such as rice, dried pasta, sugar, flour, grains)	A cool, well-ventilated dry store area	Should be kept in clean, covered containers on wheels or in smaller sealed containers on shelves to stop pests getting into them.
		Storage should be in a cool, well-ventilated dry store area; well-managed stock rotation is essential.
		Retain packaging information as this may include essential allergy advice.

Food type	Storage temperature	Storage instructions
Fish	Fridge running at 1 °C to 2 °C	A specific fish fridge is preferable. Remove fresh fish from ice containers and place on trays, cover well with cling film and label.
		If it is necessary to store fish in a multi-use fridge, make sure it is well covered, labelled and placed at the bottom of the fridge, running below 5 °C, well away from other items.
		Remember that odours from fish can get into other items such as milk or eggs.
Dairy products and eggs	Milk, cream, eggs and cheese should be stored below 5 °C. Sterilised or UHT milk can be kept in the dry store. Eggs should be stored at a constant temperature; a fridge is the best place to store them.	Milk, cream, eggs and cheese should be stored in their original containers.
		For sterilised or UHT milk follow the storage instructions on the label.
Fruit, vegetables and salad items	Dependent on type; refrigerated items should be stored at around 8 °C to avoid any chill damage.	Storage conditions will vary according to type, e.g. sacks of potatoes, root vegetables and some fruit can be stored in a cool, well-ventilated store room, but salad items, green vegetables, soft fruit and tropical fruit would be better in refrigerated storage.
Canned products	Dry store area	Cans are usually stored in the dry store area and, once again, rotation of stock is essential.
		Canned food will carry best-before dates and it is not advisable to use after this date. 'Blown' cans must never be used, and do not use badly dented or rusty cans.
		Once opened, transfer any unused canned food to a clean bowl, cover and label it, and store in the fridge for up to two days.
Cooked foods	Below 5 °C	These include a wide range of foods, e.g. pies, pâté, cream cakes, desserts and savoury flans. They will usually be 'high-risk' foods, so correct storage is essential.
		For specific storage instructions see the labelling on the individual items but, generally, keep items below 5 °C.
		Store carefully, wrapped and labelled, and well away from and above raw foods to avoid any cross-contamination.

Date marking and stock rotation

Adopt a first in – first out **(FIFO)** policy to use older stock first and observe storage (best-before) dates on packaged food. This means that a proper stock record should be kept; in many businesses a weekly stock take is done. This

can help to identify foods that are near their use-by or best-before dates so they can be used up safely.

- **Use-by dates** are given for perishable foods that need refrigeration (this must be observed by law). Any food past its use-by date must be disposed of safely. It is a criminal offence to have it on the premises.
- **Best-before dates** are provided for other items not needing refrigerated storage.

Safe preparation, cooking and holding procedures

Temperature control

Temperature plays a very important role in food safety. The temperatures between 5°C and 63°C are referred to as the **danger zone** because this is the temperature range where it is possible for bacteria to multiply, with most rapid activity at around 37°C. When cooking food, take it through the danger zone quickly. Most food should be cooked to 75°C to kill bacteria. When cooling food, cool it quickly (within 90 minutes) so that it is not in the danger zone longer than necessary.

Electronic temperature probes can be used to measure the temperature in the centre of both hot and cold food. They are also good for recording the temperature of deliveries and checking food temperatures in fridges. Make sure the probe is clean and disinfected before use (disposable disinfectant wipes are useful for this). Place the probe into the centre of the food, making sure it is not touching bone or the cooking container.

The running temperature of refrigerators, freezers and chill cabinets should be checked and recorded at least once a day. Refrigerators and chill cabinets should be below 5°C and freezers below −18°C.

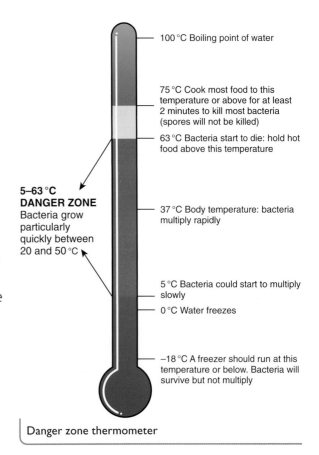

5–63°C
DANGER ZONE
Bacteria grow particularly quickly between 20 and 50°C

100°C Boiling point of water

75°C Cook most food to this temperature or above for at least 2 minutes to kill most bacteria (spores will not be killed)

63°C Bacteria start to die: hold hot food above this temperature

37°C Body temperature: bacteria multiply rapidly

5°C Bacteria could start to multiply slowly

0°C Water freezes

−18°C A freezer should run at this temperature or below. Bacteria will survive but not multiply

Danger zone thermometer

Systems are now available to log temperatures of all fridges, freezers and display cabinets in a business. Temperatures are recorded and sent to a central computer several times a day. These can then be printed or stored electronically as part of due diligence record keeping. Units not running at correct temperatures will be highlighted.

Preparation

Monitor the time that food spends at kitchen temperatures and keep this to a minimum. When preparing large amounts, do so in batches, keeping the majority of the food refrigerated until it is needed. It is important that the core temperature of food does not go above 8°C.

If you need to defrost frozen food, place it in a deep tray, cover with film and label it with what the item is and the date when defrosting was started. This is best done in a specific thawing cabinet. Alternatively, place at the bottom of the fridge where thawing liquid cannot drip on to anything else. Defrost food completely (no ice crystals on any part); once thawed, the item should remain at refrigerator temperatures and then be cooked thoroughly within 12 hours.

Cooking

Cooking food to a core temperature of **75 °C for two minutes** will kill most bacteria and these temperatures are important, especially where large amounts are being cooked or the consumers are in the high-risk categories.

However, some dishes on hotel and restaurant menus may be cooked to a lower temperature than this according to individual dish and customer requirements. Lower temperatures – but no lower than 63 °C – can be used when a whole piece of meat such as a steak is cooked. Always cook to the higher recommended temperature when meat has been boned/rolled or minced, or where the food is part of a made-up dish such as fishcakes or fish pie. The cooking temperature needs to be appropriate to ensure all **spores** are killed.

> **Professional tip**
>
> Where customers choose dishes cooked to temperatures lower than those recommended, a warning is sometimes put on the menu stating that customers eat these at their own risk.

Chilling

If food is being cooled/chilled to serve cold or for reheating at a later time, it must be cooled to **8 °C within 90 minutes**. This will help prevent multiplication of any bacteria that may be present and avoid any possible problem with spores. The best way to do this is in a blast chiller.

Freezing

If food is being frozen to be reheated at a later time, it must be frozen in a proper blast freezer. Do not put it into a normal freezer as it will not freeze quickly enough and can raise the freezer temperature. This can damage food already in the freezer. The food must be cooled to **–18 °C within 4 hours**.

Reheating

If reheating previously cooked food, reheat to at least 75 °C (the recommendation is 82 °C in Scotland). The temperature in the centre of the food must be maintained for at least two minutes and reheating must only be done once.

Holding for service, serving and transporting

Cooked food being held for service, served or transported must be kept **above 63 °C for hot food or below 5 °C for cold food.**

Food safety hazards

Food safety hazards can be categorised into the following four groups:

- **Chemical** – chemicals such as cleaning fluids, disinfectants, machine oil, insecticides, pesticides and rodenticides can accidentally get into food and make the consumer feel ill.
- **Physical** – items such as glass, nuts, bolts and oil from machinery, mercury from thermometers, flaking paint or tile grouting, pen tops, threads from worn clothing, buttons, blue plasters, hair or insects can get into foods.
- **Biological** – pathogenic bacteria, viruses, yeasts, moulds, spoilage bacteria and enzymes may be present in food. **Pathogenic bacteria** may multiply to dangerous levels but remain undetectable. If they get into the human body they can cause illness.
- **Allergenic** – the immune system in some people can react to certain foods. Allergies are usually associated with nuts, dairy products, wheat-based products (affecting those with a gluten allergy), eggs and shellfish. Some people may also have an allergy to some vegetables, plants and mushrooms. Reactions include swelling, itching, rashes and breathlessness. It may even cause **anaphylactic shock**.

> **Professional tip**
>
> A human carrier is someone carrying salmonella in their intestines but not showing any signs of illness. They can pass the salmonella on to the food they work with, which could then cause food poisoning.

Food spoilage

This is food that has spoiled or 'gone off'. Unlike contamination with bacteria it can usually be detected by sight, smell, taste or texture. Signs of spoilage include mould; slimy, over-wet or over-dry food; a sour smell or taste; discoloured and wrinkled food; or other texture changes.

It is caused by the natural breakdown of the food by spoilage organisms such as spoilage bacteria, enzymes, moulds and yeasts which, in some cases, may not be harmful themselves but cause the food to deteriorate. Spoilage may also be caused by poor storage, poor handling or by contamination of the food.

Food spoilage can account for a significant amount of unnecessary waste in a business; it should not happen if food stock is being managed and stored properly.

Any food that has spoiled or is out of date must be reported to the supervisor/line manager then disposed

of appropriately and marked 'not for human consumption'. It should be separated from general waste and be disposed of away from food storage areas.

Activity

1 What are the main differences between pathogenic bacteria and viruses?
2 What are the four requirements needed for bacteria to multiply? If they have these requirements, how quickly can they divide?
3 What is the temperature range referred to as the danger zone? Why should food be kept out of this zone as much as possible? Suggest three good working practices that will prevent food from being in this zone too long.
4 How can you check the temperature of food?
5 Show on the diagram below where you would position the following chilled foods in a multi-use fridge: raw chicken, cooked ham, cream, salmon fillets, cooked vegetable quiche, eggs, cheese, cooked pasties, pâté, fresh pasta, rump steak, milk, raw sausages, butter, frozen chicken drumsticks that need to be defrosted.

6 There is already some cream cheese in the fridge with a use-by date of today, crème fraiche with a use-by date of tomorrow and some yoghurt with a use-by date of yesterday. What should be done with these items? At what temperature should the fridge be running?
7. How is food spoilage different from food contaminated with pathogenic bacteria? Which do you think may be most dangerous and why?
8. Describe the procedures you should follow when receiving a food delivery.

Stretch yourself

1 If you know your supervisor/manager well, ask them if you can do a report suggesting ways in which the business can be made safer.
2 Write a simple training programme that could be used for a new employee to ensure that they are aware of the food safety requirements of the job.

Key words

FIFO – first in – first out, referring to using older food stocks before new deliveries.

Use-by date – these are on perishable foods that need refrigeration and must be observed by law.

Best-before date – for non-perishable foods that do not need refrigeration. It is best practice not to use the food after this date.

Danger zone – the temperature range where bacterial multiplication could take place: 5–63 °C.

Spore – a state some bacteria can achieve to survive high temperatures and disinfection.

Pathogenic bacteria – bacteria that could cause illness.

Food spoilage – food deteriorating, usually detected by taste, smell, appearance, texture, colour and so on.

Index

Page numbers in **bold** show where recipes can be found.